DOING.
BEING.
BECOMING.

DOING.
BEING.
BECOMING.

FOR THE LOVE OF THE CREATIVE ARTS

RITA EZENWA-OKORO

NEW DEGREE PRESS

COPYRIGHT © 2022 RITA EZENWA-OKORO

DOING.

BEING.   ,

BECOMING.

For the Love of the Creative Arts

ISBN   979-8-88504-595-7 *Paperback*

          979-8-88504-941-2 *Kindle Ebook*

          979-8-88504-829-3 *Ebook*

This book is specially dedicated to two extraordinary people who once graced the earth with their powerful personalities.

My late father, David Osuan Omovbude, and my late sister, Mabel Iguehi Omovbude.

This book is evidence of their influence on the girl they called Ehiaghe.

CONTENTS

———

FOREWORD		11
INTRODUCTION		15
CHAPTER 1.	MILLS AND BOONS	27
CHAPTER 2.	THE PROCESS	39
CHAPTER 3.	DEALING WITH LOSS	59
CHAPTER 4.	SHINE YOUR LIGHT	77
CHAPTER 5.	PLAY	89
CHAPTER 6.	COMMUNITY ORGANIZING	105
CHAPTER 7.	QUEEN BEE	119
CHAPTER 8.	A SPROUT IS COMING	131
CHAPTER 9.	MENTAL HEALTH	143
CHAPTER 10.	ESTRANGIER	155
CONCLUSION		167
ACKNOWLEDGMENTS		173
APPENDIX		177

Perform it until it becomes your reality.

FOREWORD

———

It is a privilege to have been asked to write the foreword for *Doing. Being. Becoming: For the love of the creative arts.* My own life and work have been spent creating ways to invite, activate, and support people to use their collective creativity to transform the global culture in humanizing ways. I find in Rita Ezenwa-Okoro a kindred spirit. I love the title of her first book because it invites the reader to imagine what it means and what they will find in its pages.

Upon reading the first chapter, readers will discover that Rita had a few goals in writing. Among them are these two: "convincing sector leaders the world over to invest more in the improvisational, experimental, experiential, 'performatory,' playful, philosophical, and probing spectrum of Creative Arts for human development," and celebrating "my steadfast love for the performing arts and the power of the creative arts as a process and result for youth leadership development." Both endear me to Rita.

I am a developmental psychologist by training. But in my life-as-lived, I am a developmentalist. I support people to develop themselves and their communities. By develop, I mean to create new responses to existing situations.

These new responses can be feelings, ways of thinking and understanding, ways of seeing and talking, and doing your relationships. Ways of responding to the scariness of the world. Ways of navigating uncertainty and unknowability. Ways of living. Ways of creating new forms of life. The world—the earth, the animals, the families—needs to develop. Without creating escape routes, we remain trapped. Without creating new things out of existing things, we continue to kill.

Rita understands this. I see it in her attitude toward young people, her founding and continuing to expand Street Project Foundation. Her proud proselytizing for play, creativity, and development is an instantiation of her understanding and of her ability to "get things done."

Rita Ezenwa-Okoro writes from the heart. Her wisdom and her creativity flow through and from her heart. Her love for and commitment to developing young people as leaders are the driving force of her courage, imagination, and determination. She understands and shares with readers the process of creating collective power and how the creative arts are necessary tools in any social change effort. She tells stories of her childhood and adolescence, sharing details of Nigerian culture. We see through Rita's eyes her development, or process of becoming: becoming a youth advocate, a creative arts practitioner, a community organizer, a developmentalist, an internationalist, and a leader in the global performance activist movement.

Rita is a powerhouse, no doubt about it. But as much as her accomplishments are impressive and inspiring, it is the developmental process she describes and illustrates that I have no doubt readers will take away and make their own.

Lois Holzman
East Side Institute, New York, NY, USA
June 25, 2022

INTRODUCTION

———

A significant part of my adolescent and teenage years was spent in Festac Town off Fifth Avenue. This town was initially referred to as Festac Village or Festival Town. It was an estate developed by the federal government of Nigeria to host forty-five thousand visitors to the World Festival of Black Arts and Culture, or FESTAC, in 1977. This world festival brought together notable musicians like the legendary Mariam Makeba from South Africa, Stevie Wonder from the United States of America, Gilberto Gill from Brazil, Mighty Sparrow from Trinidad and Tobago, Sir Victor Uwaifo from Nigeria, and many others (Bradley, 2020). I grew up in the glory days of this beautiful estate when the infrastructure was still functioning optimally before its depreciation.

I lived on a street called M Close, an enterprising community off Fifth Avenue with twenty-eight houses that lead to a dead end. The houses are neatly numbered with the odd numbers on the left and the even numbers on the right. I remember vividly all the families that occupied these houses, however, some residences became a beehive of activities and memories, which form an integral part of my childhood.

The moment you entered the close and turned left, you would see house number one. "Mama" had a convenience store set up in the garage. She was a frail old woman, knowledgeable and fluent in Yoruba but mostly communicated to her customers in Pidgin English. She was very sharp at counting her money. "Mama" would calculate her sales without a calculator and hand over your exact change. Everyone bought biscuits, *kuli kuli* (a crunchy snack made from peanuts), *baba dudu* (black sweets), and soft drinks from "Mama house one"—a colloquial way we referred to the elderly matriarchs who were resident in specific house numbers.

Across the road was house number two with its garage converted into a dry-cleaning service center where we dropped off our clothes to be picked up within two to three days. I have memories of my father looking out for the crease of his freshly starched *agbádá*. An *agbádá* is a three-piece outfit with a long-sleeved shirt, tie-up trousers, and an open-stitched gown. They are often the same color. The sharp creases on the clothes were something he looked out for after unwrapping his clothes from their dry-cleaning packaging (Migiro, 2019).

Next door to house number two was house number four, which had its garage converted into a top-class supermarket with assorted groceries. The matriarch of the house was an air hostess who did a lot of international travel, so we were sure to find imported goods on their shelf.

My friend Rosemary resided at house number six; her cousin Mercy was a hairstylist. She wove my hair when I was in secondary school. The "Evelyn King" was my favorite go-to hairstyle: *patewo* in the middle, some hair woven to the front, and some hair braided to the back. *Patewo* means "to clap your hands" in Yoruba, which references cornrows woven from left to right and right to left, meeting in the middle of your head like a mohawk. I never could tell the origins of Evelyn King hairstyle. If the 1970s disco musician inspired it, I cannot confirm.

The matriarch of house number ten traded in gold accessories. My mom bought me my first gold earrings and necklace for my tenth birthday from her. She also sold beautiful wedding gowns too.

I learned how to type because of a scholarship from the patriarch of house number eleven, Mr. Onyemere. He ran a secretarial institute. The whole ground floor was filled with IBM typewriters.

I remember Mr. Onye saw me idle one day and said, "You can come in any time you want to learn how to type." I didn't pay a dime. God bless his soul. My interest in typing and computers evolved from there.

House number thirteen was a building just beside Mr. Onye's house. The Nwochei family occupied it. The family's patriarch attended Edo College, the same secondary school as my father. I will never forget when they both discovered they were neighbors; it was a delight to watch these men reminiscing about their teenage years in secondary school. Their history solidified my friendship with Obi, Mr. Nwochei's only daughter. We weren't just neighbors; we were family friends.

Opposite house number thirteen was house number sixteen, an enterprise in and of itself thanks to my serial-entrepreneurial mother; it was home to six children and my father.

In Festac Town, the houses were semidetached duplexes with a garage to park a car and a "boys' quarters" at the back of the compound: a unique feature of postcolonial homes in Nigeria. "Boys' quarters" is a design idea imported from America, where the landowners built separate quarters for their slaves, who they considered unfit to occupy even the most uncomfortable places in the main house. It was constructed so that it faced away from the main building. In Nigeria, boys' quarters accommodated domestic help and guests, but today they have become significant assets for house owners who rent them out to the working class (Enahoro, 2013).

My mother, Elizabeth Omovbude, had such an entrepreneurial spirit that she turned the garage of the duplex where we lived into a showroom for laces, shoes, bags, and ready-made clothing. She also transformed the boys' quarters into a tailoring space that housed two industrial sewing machines, Singer machines, finishing machines, and an ironing table. The presence of sewing machines in the house triggered my interest in sewing, so I started learning. However, my interest in sewing was cut short at age twelve because we were robbed.

Due to commerce in the house, my home was an attraction for robbers, so my mom had to relocate her business. This wasn't the case for some landlords on M Close. The robbers were out to steal things of value they could easily resell, like sewing machines. So, if you were running a business in your home, you were most likely a target. Finding garages or boys' quarters converted into business centers wasn't strange. In fact, "Mama house twenty-one," a powerful woman, influencer, and leader of the close, ran a beauty salon from the garage of her home too.

Monthly meetings were organized to keep the M Close community running smoothly. Matters like the security situation were discussed. Back in the day, a neighbor who lived in house number eighteen was the secretary of the close association and owned a huge bell. Every month one of the children of the close, most often the host's child or ward, got assigned to become the town crier.

I remember I got the opportunity to be the town crier, and I would scream above my lungs with my tiny voice, "Come to the meeting at house sixteen! Come to the meeting at house sixteen!" while the bell rang. Oh my, what an experience! That bell was so heavy, and I was so tiny, but it was fun either way.

When meetings were hosted, it was a big deal. The way the landlord or landlady hosted reflected their socioeconomic status. Some homes were able to share biscuits and soft drinks. Some would go the extra mile to prepare a three-course meal for attendees, which may have included pepper soup for starters, jollof rice, fried rice with stewed chicken and *moimoi*, a delicacy made from blended bean, as the main meal, and groundnuts or *chinchin*, a crunchy pastry made from flour, for dessert. Drinks were often shared afterward.

Of all these, the most important was the sense of community, belonging, and well-being of fellow neighbors. We visited each other's homes and deliberated on pressing issues of the M Close community, like security, the welfare of the people, sanitation, and representation of members of the close at milestone events of other neighbors. The close party was one event that was sure to be discussed during the last quarter of the year.

In those days, I believed it to be the best party organized by any close community in Festac Town. During M Close parties, residents of other closes were sure to attend. A significant component of the party was the performance of the children of the close. The coordinator of the children's performances was Afoma, a dark-skinned teenager, tall and slender with a charming smile and incredible talent for dancing and organizing.

Afoma, the daughter of the secretary of the close, delighted in organizing the cultural performances of all the kids. She was a mobilizer. She ensured that as many kids as possible participated in the performance. I performed at the close party from age five until I turned twelve or thirteen. It was pretty challenging to continue performing the same way in my teenage years. The reason for this was that I was coming of age and did not want to be referred to as one of the kids anymore. This was the case with everyone else who had been a part of the performance ensemble in the early days. As they grew older, they didn't feel compelled to continue with the kids.

Cultural performances were key because we got to play dress-up and wear costumes. We spent a month of after-school rehearsals with Afoma to perfect our dance steps. We were exposed to the cultural dances of the Igbo, Yoruba, and Hausa: the major tribes in Nigeria. Thanks to our mothers, we got Ankara fabrics that we referred to as wrappers and tied them around our chests. We also made pleated skirts using George wrappers, a piece of beautiful silk fabric with gold or silver embroideries, and long fabric strands to tie them around our waist. Oh, we looked forward to wearing our costumes, holding our horsetails, and singing, "*awa de awa de*," a Yoruba song meaning, "we have come."

In hindsight, this was a rich experience for a city girl like me based in Lagos who hardly ever traveled to her hometown and state of origin of Bendel, now Edo State. Being a part of the ensemble gave me insights into our cultural differences. Besides cultural dances, we improvised drama pieces to entertain our parents. The stories we told through drama were often comical and had moral lessons. One of my go-to dances as an eight-year-old girl required that I fix both knees and palms on the ground and vigorously make up and down movements with my back and waist.

At the end of our performances, no matter how clumsy we might have been, we often received praises from our parents, expressed by throwing money or clapping vigorously as we danced.

This was the beginning of my interest in performance as youth development.

The first time there was an organized gathering with a focus on the creative industries in Nigeria was during the FESTAC celebration. Ever since then the industry has evolved in a largely unstructured manner.

Technological and economic advancements in recent years have fostered creative growth. The convergence of multimedia and mobile telecommunication technologies has led to new ways to produce, distribute, and consume content, and has in turn fostered new forms of artistic and creative expression (Maikori, 2012).

A recent survey conducted by Harris Poll on behalf of Lego shows that children in the US and United Kingdom are three times more likely to want to be YouTubers or vloggers rather than astronauts when they grow up (The Lego Group, 2019).

This aptly reflects the status quo in Nigeria and many other parts of the world. In addition, many people working in internet technology have jobs that did not exist when they were children. The youth of today may one day work jobs that no one has yet dreamed into existence. "The Next In-Demand Job Title: The Head of The Future of Work," is the title of Jena McGregor's *Forbes* article in January 2022. I found the article very intriguing because of its insight into the future of work, and I believe it validates the need to prepare our youth to become culture creators. Especially as hybrid jobs have emerged as a new normal, the world needs to create leadership to coordinate them. Inherent to the creative arts are the tools to prepare our youth for careers of the future.

According to an article published in Business Insider Africa on March 10, 2021, by Victor Oluwole:

Jobberman, Nigeria's number one career platform, has launched a new report on Nigeria's creative industry. According to the report, the creative industry is positioned as the country's second-largest employer and has the potential to produce 2.7 million jobs by 2025. Additionally, it is set to contribute 5 trillion naira to the country's GDP.

The current explosion is ignited by an ongoing renaissance, fueled by the quest for cultural identity and driven by a youthful population who are creatively inquisitive and sustained by the digital, technology, and telecoms revolution (Maikori, 2012).

Most people, however, think that creative arts are not essential to work. Creative artists or performing artists are at the bottom of the pyramid worldwide when ranked for their importance against other career jobs (Lee, 2020). In fact, creative art has long had been treated as an insignificant aspect of the country's educational program. A consequence of this neglect is visible in the fact that locally designed products remain sparce (Adedamola, Oluwafemi and Olanrewaju et al., 2021).

People don't see the value in art even when they experience it daily as comedy skits on social media or films they watch after a long day's work. More examples include creative writing by novelists that have influenced us for centuries. Songs play on our radio airwaves, keeping people's sanity together when stuck in traffic, during an aerobics routine, or serenading babies to sleep.

Colin "Alt Aesthetics" Kersley, an illustrator from the United Kingdom, states:

There has been an entrenched stigma associated with creativity in the UK for so long that it isn't considered a "real" career. Funding and educational cuts always hit the creative sector, which means that it heavily relies on individuals turning their passions into businesses with very little support. Despite all that, the creative industries contribute more to the economy than the oil, gas, automotive, sciences, and aerospace industries combined, which is pretty incredible.

The underfunding of the arts is one of the reasons I wrote this book. Stakeholders in development sectors worldwide need to understand why creative arts are crucial to young people's development and why there should be more investments in the arts. Besides, the several months of the COVID-19 lockdown inspired many people to become content creators. They used their platforms as a valuable resource for education, income, and mental health wellness.

I am compelled to write this book because my formative years in Nigeria showcase how the creative arts contributed to my development and why I have built a career in youth development. I have been a part of the creative arts industry since I was eight years old as a child model in a television commercial for Raid. The television commercial was produced by Media International: a top media company in Nigeria. Years after, I studied Creative Arts, graduating top of my class and participating in high-profile stage performances for international audiences. I also featured on television programs and did a lot of singing in church for community development and as a recording artist.

I pursued a master's degree in Media and Communications following my years as a copywriter and creative strategist across advertising agencies in Nigeria and West Africa. I founded Street Project Foundation in January 2008, a not-for-profit organization designed to use creative arts as a tool to facilitate opportunities for youth leadership development, social mobilization, and cross-cultural dialogue. In my early twenties, I started the youth movement impacting the lives of thousands of Nigerian youths directly through numerous projects like the Creative Youth Boot Camp, Digital Amazons, Street University, ARTvocacy, Talent Hub, Project RAW, Project Uplift, Haven Project, and A Smile for December.

Programming at Street Project Foundation continues until this day, intending to replicate our youth engagement models across the continent of Africa. Writing about the ideology and inspiration behind our work is the first step toward convincing sector leaders worldwide to invest more in the improvisational, experimental, experiential, performatory, playful, philosophical, and probing spectrum of creative arts for human development (Street Project Foundation, 2022).

As I began working on this book, my fortieth birthday was only nine months away, and it caused me to reflect over my life. The contemplation of what I had accomplished and what I had yet to accomplish flooded my thoughts, and suddenly, with the dexterity of a floating mind, I decided it was time to write a book. This is a book that celebrates my steadfast love for the performing arts and the power of the creative arts as a process and result for youth leadership development.

Twenty-one Sundays! This is how long I thought it would take me to write this book. Writing down my plans from my teenage years had become a thing. It was an intentional routine I engaged in at the beginning of every year, inspired by listening to preachers, motivational speakers, and life coaches, and inspirational books. The need to project my achievements for the year had become a fascination; it worked for me, I guess. My fascination with writing down my plans was inspired by the need to know what the future holds. In 2021, I decided to put aside all logic and trust God to move me to set my goals. An improvisational activity with the divine, you could call it.

Before I resolved to write a book, I had immersed myself in Lois Holzman's *The Overweight Brain* and had just begun reading President Barack Obama's *The Promised Land*. The writing style of Lois's book was quite intriguing because she broke down a very academic concept of the zones of proximal development by Lev Vygotsky, a Soviet psychologist known for his work on psychological development in children. She also expressed her postulations about the "unknown" in a relatable fashion, making me feel secure about my improvisational approach to writing this book. The uniquely written memoir of Barack Obama made me say, "Yes, I can!"

With inspirational leaders such as these, I am comfortable with my own voice and confident enough to share my development work in the creative arts field.

Doing. Being. Becoming: For the love of the creative arts shows how the creative arts are vital to youth development and how the same creative arts experiences can be applied to create other productive working spaces.

This book is for people in the development space interested in learning new ways of approaching youth development. It is also for creative arts educators and youth who want to learn more about the process of play, performance, and strategic community organizing as tools and results for revolutionary development across the world.

I hope this book helps you realize the power of the creative arts as an effective tool for your development, just like I did in my journey. I sought a clear direction, stimulating spaces, and thriving communities for doing, being, and becoming.

This book is inspirational and political. It hinges on the importance of community and the "we" factor in development. It has many personal and memorable stories from my work that inspired me.

Each chapter of this book ends with a creative exercise you can use with your youth groups. My hope is that this book helps the world realize the power of the creative arts as an effective tool for development.

CHAPTER ONE

MILLS AND BOONS

———

Caution! Romance is on my mind.

Believe it or not, my early exposure to romance novels was the precursor to developing my imaginative and creative mind.

I loved to play as a child. Who didn't? But after watching me run around the house aimlessly, my father would say, "What are you doing? Your sister has lots of books you can read to fill your time." And then he'd add in Esan, my mother tongue, "*We ya tie ebe*," or, "Go and read your book."

I did what he asked. I took his instruction as express permission to ransack boxes full of Mills and Boons and James Hadley Chase books, which were publishers of romance and detective series respectively. My eldest sister Mabel Omovbude had read and stored them all carefully years before.

In 1993, I was eleven years old, and Mabel, who is fourteen years my senior, was studying law at the University of Uyo in Nigeria and had left all her books behind when she went to school. Before I came into the picture, my elder sister Gladys, a year younger than Mabel, had also been a recipient of her legacy of romance novels. These books, which had passed on from one sister to another, were stacked in boxes and located at the top of the wardrobe in the girls' bedroom. I had to climb a stool to access the stack of books and religiously read the synopsis at the back of each book; the twisted plots influenced my book choice. Romance novels had predictable plots, but I just loved to entertain myself with their feel-good nature.

That hasn't changed! I can't watch or stay glued to a television series or movie with no touch of romance. The thought of a man and woman attracted to each other—the process of catching each other's attention, playing hard to get, conflicts like another love interest—intrigues me to this day.

I often wondered if my father knew the content of the books he was allowing his preteen daughter to bask in. Regardless, I became an adept reader because of them. I'd have a copy in my schoolbag, and in between classes in secondary school, I'd bury my head in Mills and Boons. Of course, we hid them so our teachers didn't seize them. The "we" in this instance were my classmates and I: It turned out that there was a community of Mills and Boons readers in school, and we often exchanged copies in class.

PROGRAMMING

The stories we read as children shape our minds about subjects such as race, class, relationships, hard work, discipline, and romance.

Growing up, I never saw my parents engage in any physical public display of affection. Instead, my parents gave gifts like pieces of jewelry, cars, money, the celebration of special moments like birthdays, very hearty conversations, and a shower of compliments. The Mills and Boons romance series shaped my first thoughts and imaginations about the physical display of affection in a male and female romantic relationship.

The detailed description of the male characters sucked me in because of how vivid the writers told their stories. It sometimes would go like this:

She turned and saw the dark-skinned, chiseled body of a man in his thirties, and she could tell he was the owner of the house from the pictures on the wall. Her heart was beating so fast as he walked up to her arrogantly, and he softly planted a kiss on her lips; she was astonished.

Descriptions like this were enough to make us fantasize about boys in school.

A child's nation of images evolves because of exposure. Exposure to music, dance, technology, culture, books, relationships, influences of parents, siblings, mentors, or guardians, you name it, are catalysts for our imagination. We are a sum total of our experiences, and the environment fuels the activities that stimulate our creativity.

I attended Nigerian navy secondary school Navy Town Ojo from 1991 to 1997. My literature and government teachers taught us that the romantic stories we read in these books were far from reality. We didn't understand then, as we loved to transport ourselves to a utopian world where love conquers all. Only the experience of life could teach us what genuine relationships look like. In hindsight, my constant travel through books, either romance, detective novels like James Hadley Chase, or dramatic bestsellers like Jackie Collins, were tools that helped me exercise my imaginative mind.

Children are not just inspired by what they read, but they are also intrigued by what they see; according to the American Academy of Pediatrics (AAP), "Children are influenced by media: they learn by observing, imitating, and making behaviors their own" (Alyanna, 2020).

They make deductions based on all that life throws at them, which shapes their character.

The cultivation theory postulated by George Gerbner in the 1960s validates this school of thought. It suggests that the constant exposure to media influences beliefs about the world over time (Vinney, 2019). The postulation was focused on television. Media today is vast. Anywhere a story is consumed, it is a form of media; it could be social media, books, television, films, or live performances. When we are exposed to a narrative frequently, it affects our worldview, just like my imagination about relationships was driven by my early exposure to Mills and Boons.

In like manner, Tyler Perry, an American actor, producer, screenwriter, and billionaire's life work was influenced by his family. The iconic Madea character evolved due to his abusive relationship with his father as a child. During an interview with the legendary Oprah Winfrey, Tyler narrates an ordeal with his father that made him run to his aunt, who lived around the corner. He said, "So I went to my aunt, who is one of those strong black women. She got her gun and came around to the house and put it up to his head. Her husband had to come to take the pistol from her" (Winfrey, 2010).

If you are familiar with the Madea character, you'll be able to make the connection. Perry confirmed this in an *Essence* interview when asked, "Who is Madea's character based on?"

He said, "The nurturing part of Madea comes from my mother, who would open the doors of our home to you no matter who you were. My aunt inspired the pistol-packing, the wig, and the voice. She overpronounces her words and puts an 'r' on everything to make it sound proper" (Kapusta, 2022).

Everything we need to create has been programmed in us consciously or unconsciously by our life experiences. It shapes our personalities and perceptions such that we function and perform in unique ways when faced with threats, opportunities, failures, and successes.

EXPOSURE FUELS IMAGINATION

Being the last born of the family, I grew up in a household of grown-ups. I had to find ways to make-believe. I did that through music and dance. We had audio equipment in my home in Festac Town. I played every album my father ever bought. In those days, we played music from cassettes and turntables. In the living room all by myself, I'd come up with scenarios in my head and dance until I got tired, glad that no one in my home cared to stop me from playing. I enjoyed my own company a lot. However, my Aunt Magaret, fondly called Auntie Maggi, often would come home and see my "aloneness." With my mom's permission, she would take me to my cousins' house in Ikeja, Lagos. They were around my age, so I guessed my aunt's goal was to get me to socialize, play, and relate to my peers.

"My makeup bag, my makeup bag, my my my makeup bag."

This song was composed by myself and my cousin Tina. We sang this song when we played with our Barbie dolls. My cousins traveled abroad often, and with that came lots of assorted things around their house like Barbie dolls, video games, toys, and quite a lot of things I didn't have because I had so many adults in my family home. We went swimming, to church, and to other family outings. I always had fun at my cousins' house. They lived in the Government Reserved Area in Ikeja, Lagos, Nigeria, and I was exposed to meals like chicken soup, Coco Pops, and other meals I was not accustomed to eating at home. All this exposure contributed to the nation of images stored in my mind fueled by experiences with technology, food, family, and the environment.

During the era when having a satellite dish was the "in thing," the first dish that arrived at my family house in Festac Town covered up the width of M Close and was too large for our duplex. It was all you saw, especially for a home prone to thieves. It was sure to make us easy prey. I remember that satellite dish didn't even give us many channel options. The satellite dish got changed almost immediately to another one half its size, and the world of Bop TV, CNN, TNT, you name it, was at my fingertips. I started watching channels I couldn't find on local television; thanks to the satellite, I was transported to a new world of film shows. I was only about seven years old when I had access to a world outside Festac Town.

At an early age, I had access to a part of the world I didn't know existed through the blessing of a satellite dish. I tasted meals I could only experience from my well-traveled cousins and interacted with the technology of that era with ease. Could this exposure be why I have constantly embraced the thought of global citizenship as an adult? Could this exposure to Mills and Boons be why I love romance so much?

I have been a copywriter and creative strategist for marketing communication companies in Nigeria and West

Africa for over seventeen years. One of the critical traits of a creative in advertising is a keen sense of observation. I must pick up on cultural nuances, political happenings, and trends to sponge up information to create stories told through "audio visuals," or static images with witty text, creatively put together to convince people to buy a product or service. However, during my creative process, I often draw inspiration from my past experiences, especially when working on brands for children. I worked on the Nestlé Milo brand for five years, and to sell this brand effectively, I had to be in touch with my childish side by reminiscing on my past experiences during playtime.

Ofonime Felix Okon was a child musician popularly known as "Udo Maryam," or the second son of Maryam, who played the xylophone. At the conference of Nigerian First Ladies held in Lagos, Nigeria, the late Maryam Babangida, the former first lady of Nigeria, discovered him. His performance was so electrifying that he toured the nation under the sponsorship of her pet project, Better Life for Rural Women. Over two decades later, he now manages the Udo Mariam Cultural Troupe, which his late father founded. According to Fred Iwenjora in a *Vanguard* publication on December 2019, when he asked Udo Maryam about his exposure as a four-year-old musician, he said this:

To face such a large audience at that age was an awesome event and experience. It was overwhelming at first, but my father encouraged me to go on and show them. [...] I noticed that I could play the xylophone as early as three years [old]. My late dad bought me a xylophone and sticks. He even made it possible for me to be a chief at that age [...].

Udo Maryam's father recognized his talents early and fueled them with the right tools and platforms that transformed his life and gave him a clear career path.

> ## "Minds are like parachutes; they only function when they are open."
>
> —SIR JAMES DEWAR (MODESITT JR., 2016)

I'll add to the end of this quote, "at a certain altitude." When I coach young people, I share with them this quote. For a human to have an open mind, they need exposure. Exposure turns their mind into an airplane. It allows them to fly to the altitude where they can discern the danger of a single story and explore different perspectives even after they have already developed an opinion.

Exposure shouldn't be a luxury but a necessity. Exposure is being aware, being present, and interacting with the world in many creative ways.

Exposure is fuel for the imagination and the catalyst for vision, creativity, understanding, and communication.

Besides integrating a rich Creative Arts curriculum into early childhood education, cultural exchange programs are necessary. As much as in-person exchanges are my most preferred approach, with technology, we can create virtual forums where kids can interact with their peers across borders. These exchange programs will expose children to the beauty of our diversity. We are social beings, and early exposure to the things that make us different, like our talents, belief systems, ethnicity, language, accents, and nuances, is important. Including the things that make us similar, like our needs, aspirations, struggles, physical attributes, and health, should be paramount.

Children should also be encouraged to read. Reading exercises our capacity to imagine, a skill needed for problem-solving and a life skill for the future of work. There is a famous proverb that says: "A child who reads will be an adult who thinks."

My exposure to Mills and Boons, television, relationships with family and friends, belief systems, and opportunities to travel have programmed me to be a change agent. We need more social change-makers in the global south so that we can solve our unique challenges using methods that work for us.

It is about time that the poorest countries of the world, which often come from the continent of Africa, invest in inspiring a generation of young people who are exposed and skilled enough to imagine a better world. Leadership in government are in a unique position to make the internet accessible to everyone and develop sustainable resource centers where the youth have unlimited access to the world through books, videos, and augmented reality.

According to an Economic Commission for Africa report in February 2017:

The 2030 Agenda for Sustainable Development and Agenda 2063 underscore the importance of promoting rights of young people and meeting their needs in all their diversity. Engaging young people is central to the successful implementation of the transformative agenda in Africa. Accordingly, achieving these aspirations requires an understanding of the needs, interests, challenges, and potentials of Africa's youth. The present report aims to provide a resource for formulating and implementing policies that promote engagement, empowerment, and investment in young people in Africa.

For these policies that have been formulated to work at a grassroots level, it depends on the amount of exposure we create for our youth today through affordable internet access and exchange programs designed by schools, the government, and corporate organizations. Systems need to be developed for consistent capacity building for the African youth through funded mechanisms that expose them to people from different countries, cultural backgrounds, and ideologies. It would even be better if the exposure created aligns with the youths' talents, interests, and life's purpose. This singular act will open up their horizon and make them co-creators of a society where the systems created work for their communities.

I am a beneficiary of an exchange program called the Mandela Washington Fellowship for Young African Leaders, or YALI, a program funded by the United States government. This initiative was made possible by the visionary leadership of President Barack Obama, the former President of the United States of America. As a result of this initiative, I have friends in Cameroon, the Gambia, Senegal, the Democratic Republic of the Congo, Zambia, South Africa, Niger, Kenya, and the United States of America to mention a few.

Initiatives of this nature should be replicated or built upon by the African Union and institutionalized to address the ongoing concern of youth leadership development in the continent of Africa. We do not have to wait for the economic giants to shape the Africa of our dreams. We need to shape our dreams with the might and minds of our youth. This can be achieved by creating environments where a young girl in a rural community in Emaudo, Ekpoma, in Edo State, Nigeria, has the opportunity to see a world that is different from her current reality. This exposure will open her mind to a whole new world of possibilities that will make her hunger for the transformation of her community.

In the words of one of my favorite comedians:

> "We tell people to follow their dreams, but you can only dream of what you can imagine and, depending on where you come from, your imagination can be quite limited."

—TREVOR NOAH, *BORN A CRIME: STORIES FROM A SOUTH AFRICAN CHILDHOOD* (NOAH, 2016)

Let's do all we can to burst open the imagination of the African youth by exposing them to a world that is different from their own. By so doing, we provoke their minds to start creating and transmitting the nation of images they have gathered in their subconscious through an artistic language that is second nature to them. These forms of creation can be transmitted through poetry, music, dance, drama, visual arts, comedy, and various forms of storytelling. As a result, we build a collective of youth leaders who become culture creators who can disrupt the status quo by creating something new and effective for now and the future.

Let's stretch the imagination of your youth with this exercise:

THE GIVING GAME

1. Form a big circle.
2. Tell your youth group to each take a turn to create a gift that they will hand over to someone next to them.
3. Tell them to play with their facial expressions and make body movements when creating their gifts.
4. As they create their gifts, tell them to share a story about the gift they are creating and hand over the gift without mentioning what the gift is.
5. The recipient of the gift must exaggerate facial expressions and mention what they have received. For example, with exaggerated surprise and excitement, they might say, "Oh my, thank you for this round-trip ticket to the Bahamas! I have been longing for this opportunity."
6. After receiving the gift, the recipient of the last gift starts to create a new imaginary gift for the next person in the circle while telling a story.
7. Please keep it going until everyone in the group has had a go at it.
8. After completing the activity, have the youth reflect on the process of their performance.

CHAPTER TWO

THE PROCESS

_____

The process is unknowable until
you embark on the journey.

"How is your work developing you?"

Barbara Silverman, a social therapist and founder of Developing Across Borders from the East Side Institute, New York, asked me this question after I made a presentation titled "Theatre of the Unknowable," at the virtual edition of the Performing the World Conference in 2020. It was a presentation about the process of co-creating productions with our youths using a social therapy tool we call "Reflection Sessions," which is an improvisational method of creating immersive stories with the youth who undergo training at the creative youth boot camp organized by the Street Project Foundation.

The Street Project Foundation is a youth-focused not-for-profit organization I founded in 2008. It was born out of a burning desire to use creative arts as a tool for youth leadership development, social mobilization, and cross-cultural dialogue. Since its inception, we've run numerous capacity-building workshops and boot camps for development.

Social therapeutics is a social and cultural approach to human learning and development, not a biologically scientific approach. As a philosophically informed, practically oriented "practice of method," social therapeutics relates to human beings not as behaving individuals who only adapt to culture, but as culture creators and ensemble performers of their lives (East Side Institute, 2022).

Fred Newman originated this school of thought in the 1970s.

The Performing the World Conference was born following conversations between East Side Institute's co-founders Lois Holzman and Fred Newman. This happened at a time when they had discovered performance and its essential role in human development. The conference has since become a platform where scholars, performing artists, clowns, musicians, educators, medical doctors, therapists, and many more converge to share their theories on play and performance. This conference is a unique community where people gather together to "perform a new world" (Performing the World, 2022).

When I was a student of the International Class of East Side Institute, I had the opportunity to observe Barbara Silverman's group social therapy sessions in person and online, and I always found her questions thought-provoking and disruptive in a good way.

When she asked the question, "How is your work developing you?" I paused and reflected on how far I had come and how much I had accomplished. Reflecting on how my work developed me required more thinking. I immediately realized that I had been self-absorbed in my career for so long and had not taken a step back to assess the holistic effect of my work on my life as a human being. I thought about the numerous activities I had been doing and the milestones that triggered the development of the Street Project Foundation.

CREATING SPACE

In December 2013, I was recovering from a major heartbreak: the ending of a nine-year relationship that had no definition and direction, but which I'd hoped would lead to an "I do." Those Mills and Boons stories were still fresh in my mind. You'll understand the feeling if you've been dumped over WhatsApp for another woman. I decided to embark on a one-month vacation in the United States of America to clear my head. The first half of the holiday was spent with my cousin and his family in California. I'm glad I got to experience the cool weather in Cali in the winter! The second half of my vacation was spent in the Bronx, New York, with my uncle and his family. It was a white Christmas in New York that year, and so I got to experience snow and true cold for the first time.

My uncle's humble apartment was home to me for the last two weeks of my vacation, and it was in that apartment that I truly put the heartbreak behind me. It came after reading a Bible verse following desperate prayers for God to give me a word to enable me to move on with life.

"For the vision is yet for an appointed time, but at the end, it shall speak, and not lie: though it tarry, wait for it; because it will surely come, it will not tarry."

—HABAKUK 2:3 (KJV)

It was a clear word from God that though my desire for a life partner had been delayed at thirty-two years old, I should wait for it; it would come to pass. This scripture became my anchor and faith booster. I thought there was something wrong with me when the heartbreak happened. I wasn't myself, and it was difficult to think past my pain and focus on my professional life. So, a period of isolation and departure from the environment I was used to was a great opportunity to commune with God; I received a revelation for my next move. With this pain out of the way, I was able to think straight and continue to be my adventurous self again. I decided to find an organization in the United States that worked in the same field as the Street Project Foundation— the fostering of creative education in young people—and check them out in hopes of brokering partnerships.

CONCEPTION STAGE

The process of the Street Project Foundation's development can be likened to a mother nurturing her baby from infancy to its teenage years.

I had the opportunity to work as a tutor, speech therapist, and supervisor at a start-up foundation called Learning Interventions before I embarked on my National Youth Service Corps, or NYSC, which is a mandatory one-year service to Nigeria. Learning Interventions was owned by a Caucasian woman from the United States living with a physical disability, married to a top bank executive who was posted to Nigeria. She moved down to Nigeria with her three beautiful kids; one, in particular, was very special. Eddie was a three-year-old boy on the autism spectrum with a fascination for shoes and doors opening and closing.

Working with Eddy was as developmental for me as it was for him. It was also a lucrative job. I was paid by the hour. It was so lucrative that I bought my first Trium-brand mobile phone in the first month of starting the job. In the year 2002, mobile phones were new in Nigeria; buying a phone was expensive, and phone calls were billed by the minute and not per second. I followed Eddy to school on some days so I could guide him in class and get him to socialize as much as possible with other kids in the school. On other days, I worked with him at home on a strict schedule. There was time for play, snacks, and cognitive learning. I had tools like a gum massager to stimulate his jaws, flashcards to develop his cognitive skills, and toys to stimulate curiosity. Eddy was a fun kid to hang out with. It was a job that required both my undivided attention, spontaneity, and creativity.

One day, Eddy climbed the wardrobe to get the lollipop I used for reinforcements during my sessions for cognitive learning. He climbed up and put the lollipop in his mouth but couldn't get back down because he was hanging on the third tier of the wardrobe while I was chatting with his mom in another room in the large apartment.

We heard him scream for help, and his mom and I walked in to see what Eddy had been up to. We burst out laughing. I grabbed him and used his desire for the lollipop as an opportunity to work on his cognitive skills and reward him after a job well done. Unfortunately, my Trium phone was not smart enough to capture such hilarious moments, but if social media were a thing then, it would have gone viral. #KidsDoTheDarndestThings.

These sorts of things happened often, and I learned to build with what Eddy offered as I worked with him. Years later, I could see how the Street Project Foundation required that we build on what the youth offered to the group, just like little Eddy. Being attentive, creative, and spontaneous made our engagement with the youth organic and customized for different youth groups.

Following my work with Eddy, I got a second job working with a two-year-old named Oki, the smartest kid I had ever worked with. All I needed to do was read him a book once and he would memorize the whole thing and recite it back to me without looking. Oki didn't make eye contact, and this affected his ability to socialize. He zoned out very quickly, and it was challenging working with him. I remember vividly the first time Oki said, "I love you," to his mom without being prompted. Her eyes brightened up, and she hugged him. She was very grateful for the work I was doing with her son.

LEARNING FROM THESE LITTLE ONES

I was twenty years old then, so working with these special kids was an eye-opener for me. I realized that all the kids I was fortunate to have worked with had well-to-do parents; however, despite their wealth, they still struggled to care for children with learning disabilities. When a condition inhibits the developmental process of a child, the parents also feel like they are going through a similar form of disability. Until they find a solution to facilitate the process of growth for their children, they don't stop, regardless of how wealthy or resourceful they might be. It made me understand that some people need more care than others for them to develop, and we must be empathetic, patient, and thankful for the progress made.

At the time, I didn't realize that my work with people with disabilities at this stage of my career would become a significant component of my work at the Street Project Foundation. Development is central to human existence and sustainability. The day we stop developing, we die. As such, I was opening up to the experience of working with a child on the autism spectrum or with cerebral palsy as my way of sponging up what would in turn help me develop the Street Project Foundation.

MOVING ON AND MOVING OUT

After six months of working as a tutor, it was time to resume the National Youth Service Corps camp at Ipaja, Lagos, Nigeria. Eddy's mom and Oki's mom were particularly disappointed that I had decided to leave. They were willing to have me spend my youth service year working with their kids, but I had already asked myself this question: Would I be fulfilled in ten years doing this job? It had served its purpose for me. I didn't connect with the job like it was my life's purpose, and I still felt I had a lot to explore before making a firm career decision. I learned that even though a job pays well and feels suitable for a period, that doesn't mean it's your life's purpose. In addition, in making tough decisions, you will hurt people. You will sometimes dash their dreams for you but what is essential is that you don't dash your dreams for yourself. It's your life, and you come first because you are the main character in your own life journey.

I turned twenty-one years old on the day I reported at the Youth Service campground. I had to join the long queue under the scorching sun to undergo verification and get my camp uniforms. It wasn't how I pictured spending my first day as an adult. Though eighteen is the legal age in Nigeria, I considered twenty-one the end of my teens and the beginning of adult benefits and worries. I felt like I had come of age and accomplished much being in this campground at twenty-one, ready to take on the world.

Ideally, I wanted to celebrate this day differently; it was my birthday but being a youth corp member was also a thing of pride. It was a symbol of my accomplishment as a university graduate. Wearing the khaki uniform and orange boots and being hailed "Corper Shun," a salutation to a youth corp-er, was an experience I wanted to go through, having seen my siblings go through the same. I got to wear their National Youth Service Corps branded T-shirts as hand-me-downs long before I even became a youth corp-er.

The way the youth service corp worked was that after three weeks of intense camp activities, the youth were deployed to work in organizations in a local government area of the state. In that local government, you were expected to report for Community Development Service once a week.

At the Youth Service camp, I joined the drama department. It was only to be expected because I studied creative arts, and my natural inclination was to participate in any artistic endeavor. My platoon participated in a theatre competition and came third. I had made a couple of friends who were like-minded, and they had ideas.

Unlike the other youth corp-ers, who were expected to serve in various local governments, my creative friends in the camp wanted to do a type of community service that was also an opportunity to do what they loved: perform music. They proposed this idea to the camp authorities, and it was approved. With this arrangement, we didn't have to report for community service at the local government area councils like the others. Instead, we reported to the Youth Service Secretariat in Surulere, Lagos. The Special Community Development group was a music group we called the ONE HOUSE Music Unit.

I was torn between joining this new movement and going with an already established drama group, which also operated at the Lagos Headquarters. As a person who loves to pioneer ideas and activities, I was intrigued by the thought of joining a grouping of boxless-thinking youth to start something new. I joined the ONE HOUSE Music Unit and became its first Vice President. It was one of the best decisions I had ever made. This is because of my one year of writing songs on social justice, jamming and composing those songs with an ensemble of musicians, and going under Ojuelegba Bridge and Ikeja Bridge (both densely populated commercial centers in Lagos, Nigeria) to perform, which positively affected my thinking faculty.

A seed was sown in my heart while we were spreading the word about the need for unity in the nation and the importance of putting an end to ethnic rivalry, corruption, and violence. From that day onward, I could not stop thinking about the intersections between the creative arts, social justice, and human development. I kept brooding on how creative arts could be utilized beyond its entertainment value as a force for social transformation in Nigeria.

At the time, I had never heard of any creative arts inclined not-for-profit organization using creative art forms for social transformation. As such, the thought of developing the idea of the Street Project Foundation was groundbreaking. The state of creative development in Nigeria was comatose and hopeless for a Creative Arts graduate from the University of Lagos. Remember the Second World Festival of Black Arts and Culture in 1977 that I wrote about in the introductory chapter? What I didn't state was the fact that a National Arts Theatre and National Council for Arts and Culture were both established for the festival. These were solid infrastructure for the creative development of Nigeria.

In 2002, when the idea of the Street Project Foundation was brooding, the National Theatre was dilapidated, and National Council for Arts and Culture was a shadow of what it once was, a vibrant sector. According to a *Business Day* publication by Hope Moses-Ashike and Emelike Obinna in April 2022:

It is no longer news that the National Theatre in Iganmu, Lagos, which is a foremost Nigerian historic monument and supposedly creative industry hub, has been in ruins for the major part of the forty-five years it has been in existence.

Besides the Nollywood and music industry, the creative development of Nigeria was struggling in 2002, and investments in the use of the arts as a tool for human development were very limited.

A thread that cuts through the co-creation of the ONE HOUSE Music Unit and the process of developing the Street Project Foundation is, first, a sense of community. Collaborating with like-minded creatives was a visionary breakthrough. In the same fashion, when the idea of the Street Project Foundation started to crystalize in my mind, I had to find people with similar passions. Secondly, we were performers and improvisers at the ONE HOUSE Music Unit, and the same DNA runs through the Street Project Foundation's programming. Above all, the need to be change agents was at the heart of our performances, and the same rings true for the Street Project Foundation.

INCUBATION

After we completed our Youth Service Corps, I celebrated my 22nd birthday with five thousand naira or the equivalent of thirty-six US dollars. Don't laugh. I remember vividly telling my entire household I would celebrate my 22nd birthday since I didn't get to celebrate my 21st birthday.

My father asked, "How much do you have?"

I said, "I have five thousand naira."

In my heart, I knew five thousand naira could only rent the canopy and chairs; however, this was my usual tactic of getting my dad to support my vision. As manipulative as this may seem, this is a critical lesson for entrepreneurs. If you have a vision that you cannot save for or put your own money into, how do you think an investor will decide to invest in your venture?

I didn't know this was the principle I was deploying, but it worked. My five thousand naira had many more zeros added to it to take care of food and fuel for the "I beta pass my neighbor"* generator; invitations were sent out to all my friends, and voila! I celebrated my birthday. It was somewhat of a farewell to all my Youth Service Corps friends, specifically those I had bonded with at ONE HOUSE Music Unit. They were a significant force in my life that impregnated the vision of the Street Project Foundation in my heart.

After completing my youth service year, I tried to replicate the same community intervention model for evangelical purposes. I assembled all my friends with voices: Eduvie, Tayo, and three others who loved to sing and were Christians. We took our music to the streets. We called it Street Praise. After a couple of months of doing this and recording two original

---

*   "I beta pass my neighbor" is an informal way we Nigerians refer to a mini generator. This is how we say that "despite the size of my generator, I am in a better position than anyone who is without a generator due to the epileptic electric power supply in Nigeria."

songs in the studio, I knew this wasn't what I honestly had in mind; it was still a shadow of what was coming.

Like most young people after tertiary education, the priority after so many years in university was getting a job and building a career. I got to focus on that after my Youth Service year and while I worked in advertising in the year 2004, I was nurturing the idea first as Street Praise.

I spent 2007 reflecting on what I wanted to grow with this seed in my heart. I paused on Street Praise and, with the help of Barrister Femi Austin Chigbu, who I asked to register Street Praise, a conversation ensued.

"We can't register this entity with the word 'praise' in it," Barrister Chigbu said.

"Why won't it fly?" I asked.

He said, "Praise gives a connotation that it is a religious institution."

I told him, "I don't want to register a religious institution."

He said, "I know. I advise we change 'praise' to 'project.' It's nice."

After a little consideration, I said, "Okay, let's do this!"

This was how Street Project was registered as an enterprise. It was expensive registering the organization as a nonprofit at the time, so I settled for a business name registration first, which was less expensive.

I started writing down everything I wanted Street Project to become. One thing I remember writing down was that I wanted to build an organization that could sustain itself. At the time, I wasn't familiar with the concept of social entrepreneurship. It was relatively a new concept at the time, especially with the world's commitment to development goals.

Businesses were inspired to run a sustainable model where the focus was not just on making a profit but also on solving a social problem. It was a business for profit and for social good. I knew I wanted the Street Project Foundation to be about youth development with creative arts at its core in response to the massive unemployment rate and a prevailing culture of wasted years in Nigerian universities studying courses that were not in line with young people's innate gifts. I thought about the youth creating products like hoop earrings, dope jeans, and hip tees that could be sold for the youths' economic benefit and the organization's sustainability. I was also clear that I wanted to work with vulnerable youth who did not have the means to access the kind of creative arts projects I wanted to design.

With the very alarming youth unemployment rate, I sought to find an alternative way to solve the problem youth faced as a result of a lack of employment, mentors, and community.

According to the latest labor force report of the National Bureau of Statistics, unemployment among young Nigerians aged fifteen to thirty-four years old is the highest in the country, with 21.72 million or 42.5 percent of the 29.94 million young Nigerians in the labor force unemployed. For comparison, the national unemployment rate stood at 33.3 percent as of December 2020 (Ochayi, 2022).

I wrote down what I wanted the organization's structure to look like long before I employed my first staff member. I wrote down what I could afford to start doing immediately and what I absolutely could not start doing based on my limitations.

Writing down one's vision gives clarity. It does not mean that everything you have written down will automatically begin to take shape, but it helps you put things in proper perspective. Writing down your vision is a prerequisite for planning the future. If you can see it, you can design it, implement it, and then achieve it.

> "Vision without action is a daydream.
> Action without vision is a nightmare."

—A FAMOUS JAPANESE PROVERB (WOOD, 2020)

I met Chuka Obi at SO&U Saatchi and Saatchi, an advertising agency I worked in at the time, and I requested that he sketch out my vision of the logo of the Street Project Foundation. I held on to that drawing in black and white for a year before it even got colored digitally. Every time I stared at the sketched logo, it inspired me to craft structures and models that were beyond my current scope. As I began to see the vision of what the organization could become in my mind, I felt compelled to sell it. Facebook had become a thing at the time, so I took advantage of the platform and started to share pictures of events I had organized.

THE BIRTH OF THE STREET PROJECT

My first project for Street Project was called "A Smile for December," a project christened by Marcia Anagor, my colleague at the advertising agency. Just like childbearing, the birthing process cannot be done alone.

I was selling the vision so well that I had begun gathering allies in my workplace. Chuks Anagor was intrigued by the vision and was quite sure his wife Marcia would buy into the idea, and she did. Marcia then shared the vision with Michael, a talented singer. All I needed was just one person to believe in the vision I had conceived, and I had three. They loved the idea of using the arts for youth development, being singers themselves. However, there was just one challenge: I didn't have any money to implement the kind of project I had envisioned.

Michael brought up working with orphanages, and I loved it. Working in advertising meant I was resourceful when creating flyers for projects. Facebook became my first office for Street Project, and I ran my first fundraiser on the platform. I sold branded T-shirts in my office and on Facebook. I got people to donate toward our visit to Heart of Gold Hospice in Surulere, Lagos. We had a party there and shared music, cakes, food, and love with them.

Coincidentally, this home is one where children with learning disabilities are sheltered, and it was so easy to connect with every child because of my experience with learning disabilities. Reflecting on the connections between both institutions made me realize that no experience is wasted. We go through experiences to gain the maturity to handle them even better when confronted with similar circumstances.

"No experience is wasted. Everything in life is happening to grow you up, to fill you up, to help you become more of who you were created to be."

—OPRAH WINFREY

After the first activity at Heart of Gold Children's Hospice, we visited orphanages every year for five years. However, in 2010, three years after our activities kicked off, we launched our first youth project called *"Project Raw,"* a talent hunt competition. Project Raw was the idea I had conceived three years before that I did not have sufficient funds to implement. This was the beginning of many more youth interventions that have catalyzed thousands of youths to discover their full potential and activate them for social good.

"HOW IS YOUR WORK DEVELOPING YOU?"

As simple as that question was, it shook me to my core. It woke me up to the realization of the need to self-reflect always. There's a tendency for development workers to be so selfless that they forget about making time for themselves. So, I spent a day reflecting on this question, and the one word that resonated with me was **capacity**.

> "We don't even know how strong we are until we are forced to bring that hidden strength forward. In times of tragedy, of war, of necessity, people do amazing things. The human capacity for survival and renewal is awesome."
>
> —ISABELLE ALLENDE (ALLENDE, 2022)

I discovered that the journey toward developing the Street Project Foundation was my resilience voyage. In building resilience, I was growing. I evolved to becoming a community organizer, a project manager, a fundraising strategist, a marketer, a social entrepreneur, a visionary leader, a movement builder, a communications manager, a risk-taker, and a human resource manager.

When I dared to perform a revolutionary activity, I became like an elastic band, capable of stretching my faculty. This question was a call to the awareness of who I was being and becoming due to my fearless expedition to the land of the unknown called the Street Project Foundation. There were failures along the way, but I persevered.

> "I believe that the only courage anybody needs is the courage to follow your own dreams."
>
> —OPRAH WINFREY (WINFREY, 2022)

It certainly took courage to embark on this revolutionary activity. I remember the first volunteer I recruited was a young man who came to my office often at Quest Publicis Advertising to sell books. I engaged his services to support the delivery of letters to corporate organizations for our social interventions in orphanages. At the initial stages of our youth programming, we focused on talent competitions, but I quickly realized that if this was about human development, we must find effective ways to build a community around the strengths of the youth that signed up for our programs.

At the early stages of Street Project Foundation's development, we didn't do well with tracking our impact; as such I had many meetings with gatekeepers in the development sector that fell flat because I didn't understand the process of securing such high-level partnerships. However, there was no doubt in my mind that we were on to something revolutionary and that embracing the failures and successes in the course of its development was essential.

Revolutionary activity is one of the constructs in social therapeutics inspired by Marx, a German philosopher, and Vygotsky, a Soviet psychologist, that human beings are both determined by the existing circumstances *and* have the capacity to transform these circumstances into something new (East Side Institute, 2022).

It has been fourteen years since the dream of a creative youth movement was in motion. Every year we create, design, build, and replicate ideas; my mind, emotions, skill set, and spirituality are stretched. This gives me the ability to do a range of things outside my comfort zone.

Now we are breaking new grounds beyond the city of Lagos. Replication of our models across other parts of Nigeria and sub-Saharan Africa has become a priority. Street Project Foundation is now a part of a global community that supports with training and mentorship thanks to the East Side Institute, The Global Play Brigade, and the Performing the World Community.

In all of these, what has been most important is enjoying the process. Patience, they say, is a virtue, and in any career, a lot of patience must be exercised. The best way to manage the wait is to embrace the process as an essential component of the result. Celebrating wins as simple as recognizing how you have developed as a result of the process is necessary.

So, I'll ask you this same question: How is your work developing you? Take some time to reflect on your journey as a development practitioner. Be present and aware of what you are being and becoming.

The following activity exercises the mind and develops the youths' critical thinking skills. Our focus is always on the process and not necessarily the overall result of a perfect speech. It strengthens their confidence and gives them the freedom to be silly in the process such that they might lose their train of thought during the speech, but the beauty would also be seen in how they navigate their way back to the core topic.

SPONTANEOUS SPEECHES

1. Write a series of topical and social issues on pieces of paper. (Inclusion, inequality, unemployment, police brutality, etc.)
2. Fold them so no one can see them beforehand.
3. Set your stage. Include a podium or a raised platform to give your youth an illusion that they are speaking to a crowd of people.
4. Get a volunteer to pick from the pool of topics.
5. Get them to read it out and then breathe in through their nose and out through their mouth before they start their spontaneous speech.
6. Encourage the audience to celebrate the volunteer on stage before they begin.

CHAPTER THREE

DEALING WITH LOSS

Brace yourself; it's about to get emotional.

Grief is developmental.

I was thirteen years old when Mabel died. She was the first child of my mother. My father called her his crown.

Her position in the family was very significant because of the natural leadership role she assumed as the first of six children. Mabel was a very beautiful woman. She was very particular about her looks and her hair. I looked up to her. I wanted to be a lawyer because she studied law. My vision of her inspired my current fascination for hair highlights. She loved fashion so much that she specifically designed one of the dresses I wore on my tenth birthday. She was an organizer and a planner. She was also steadfast and confident. When she walked into a room, you couldn't miss her. Her charisma was second to none.

Mabel and I were movie buffs. She particularly loved sending me to the video club because she felt I had a knack for selecting the best films. Back in the day, VHS cassettes were the order of the day. Movie choices were often made based on the title and a movie poster. She took after my father's oratory skills, so you wanted to listen to her accent when she spoke. It was a mixture of an American accent she picked up while initially studying in the United States of America and a polished Nigerian British accent. She also loved taking me to church. I was her baby sister; she loved me, and I loved her too.

In my family, we struggle with our weight, and my late sister was not left out of the struggle. Most of her body fat was concentrated on her buttocks, but no one else in the family had that same body shape. For some reason, back in the day, people felt to lose weight on their butt, they had to slam it on the wall. I'm not joking; my late sister would slam her butt on the wall. The thought of it makes me crack up laughing. I do not know if it ever worked. Besides that, I looked up to her; I miss her.

Her absence created a vacuum in my life. She was forward-thinking, and I believe she would have made great strides in life. Setting the pace spiritually, materially, maritally, and financially ahead of my siblings and me, she influenced the family's growth. She was creative.

She passed down her Mills and Boons romance novels from generation to generation the same way she passed down her clothes. Her clothes were beautiful. They were tailor-made. She would buy her fabrics and design the exact style she wanted. I was the one she would send to pick up her dresses from the tailor. I loved her style. I just loved her as a person. Unfortunately, our relationship was cut short by death.

Losing my sister and dealing with death is one of the things that made me hang on to my Christian faith and belief in a superior being. The year of her passing was when I truly gave my life to Christ. I was exposed to the teachings of pastors and leaders whose messages focused on not wasting your youth. The exposure to how fickle life is made me understand that we have no time to waste here on Earth. This resonated with me at the time, and it became essential to me to not waste my youth because time's too short. I needed to get things done and not procrastinate. This was my motivation, and it took the passing of a loved one very early in my teenage years to make me understand the importance of time.

> "Time is a created thing. To say 'I don't have time' is to say 'I don't want to.'"
>
> —LAO TZU (OGBO, 2021)

I find this quote by the ancient Chinese philosopher and writer, Lao Tzu, so striking. I can say confidently that you too have used the "I don't have time" excuse just as much as I have. For instance, I had many reasons why I couldn't have written this book, especially with the numerous programs I manage, the consultancy services I provide to businesses, and my commitment and devotion to family time. I simply did not have the time; I had to create the time because I wanted to get my first book published.

There were many emotional high and low moments that would have stopped me from completing this project. Fundraising for this book took me out of my comfort zone, but sheer will kept me going. I slipped on my deadlines many times, but it was the desire to get it done for the sixty-one people who believed in me enough to invest in the idea of me writing a book that really drove me.

There will always be high and low moments in our lives that make our emotions gallop like the waves of an ocean. Today a loved one is alive and cheerful; tomorrow, they are no more. Today you have a job that pays the bills; tomorrow, the bills are piling up with no earnings to pay them off. Today, you're healthy; tomorrow, you're not. There is a reason why life isn't straightforward. The ups and downs of life were designed to work patience and strengthen resilience in us.

There are vast differences in the way that children and adults grieve, namely because children have not yet developed complex and abstract reasoning skills to express and understand their feelings and emotions (Slate and Scott, 2019).

One of the best and most natural ways that children and adolescents express themselves is through art. Painting, drawing, sketching, coloring, and writing are just a few creative modalities that can help children release and make sense of heavy and confusing emotion (Gidlund, 2022).

The creative arts give young people the tools to manage their emotions, and I share with you through my stories just how experiences of grief can be a catalyst for developing feelings and a positive attitude to life.

Until you've been through challenging situations, you'll never know the superpower you carry as a human being. This chapter looks into the performance of emotions that help us become "doing" individuals. In the process of doing, we investigate the force that emotions born out of grief provide in creating revolutionary activities for the holistic development of the human race.

Empowerment cannot be achieved through spoon-feeding young people, treating them as a passive audience for lectures. Young people become empowered through doing things themselves: telling their stories, sharing their dramas, drawing their lives and discussing and analysing these issues, looking for solutions, and planning with their peers what can be done to change things. Active and learner-centered methods enable young people to make sense out of their experiences and build critical thinking skills that help them take more control of their lives (UNESCO, 2010).

I have always found it most effective to not tell young people what to do but trigger them to figure out what to do themselves. One of our Street Project Ambassadors, who was used to a pattern of being told what to do because of her frequent exposure to psychologists and therapists, found it unnerving during reflection sessions to have a lot of people pour out their emotions and not get a solution from me. I remember stating emphatically that the solution lies within them and within the community. I said, "We are not in the telling game here."

Our programs are designed to strengthen your capacity as a youth to think and make well-thought-out decisions. When emotions are high, we use tools like writing or making works of art, and through these methods, the youth create the future they want for themselves. These artistic formats set them on a path to reflecting on their next steps. The Street Project Ambassador in question gradually figured out what our convenings were about and got out of her comfort zone and shared so many powerful stories that were performed on stage during their showcase.

According to President Hennessy's annual address to the Academic Council of Stanford University, April 20, 2006,

"In addition to the role of the arts in fostering creative thinking, the arts give us a venue for dealing with the complexities and ambiguities of human existence."

The creative arts provide an alternative universe in the form of play, where we can get the youth to freely express themselves without judgment and reflect in a way that makes them self-aware of pain and intentionally find ways out of the dark spaces. They can do this by forming positive habits with the help of a curator and grouping the youth with like minds.

Research shows that around half of our daily actions are driven by repetition. This is probably why behavioral scientists and psychologists have spent so much time writing about establishing and keeping positive habits (DePaul, 2021).

Habits are formed through regular repetition until they become second nature to you. To cultivate a habit, you must be able to repeat that activity for three weeks and then continue for another ninety days (DePaul, 2021).

Forming positive new habits can be challenging, and getting rid of old negative habits even tougher, hence the need for a trigger or motivation. This is where grief comes in. It might not necessarily be the loss of a loved one. It could be the loss of a job, a divorce, failure of an examination, health crisis, sudden disability, delays in child conception, or a miscarriage. As long as it causes pain and places you in a desperate situation or an unfamiliar territory, that grief can help you discover your strength and drive change to happen.

DEALING WITH THE LOSS OF HEALTH

Besides experiencing the loss of a loved one at an early age, I was also dealing with a goiter diagnosis, a condition in which the thyroid gland grows significantly. I had emaciated in weight so much that my eyes were bulging out, and

I didn't look pretty. My skin color became very washed out and dark, what people would call dirty black, because I was always sweating profusely. These symptoms were evident before I was diagnosed.

My parents didn't know what was happening, as I began to get sick when I was in boarding school at age eleven. The moment they realized how sick I had become, I had to be taken out of boarding school and became a day student, which meant I wasn't living in the school hostel or boarding school. After school was over in the day, I returned home. Following my admission to Eko Hospital in Lagos, I was diagnosed with a goiter. I was pumped with a lot of medication to manage my thyroid gland. Gradually, I started gaining weight and got better.

During the period of what I'll call an "affliction," I lost a lot of friends. As a girl, I understood early in life how vain humans could be. Judgment is placed on you based on how you look and what you wear as opposed to the value you can offer or what you have within you. This is prevalent even more in the era of social media, where loads of people hide behind their phones, spilling vile things to make themselves feel better. When awful things are said about you, there's sure going to be a whirlwind of emotions stirring up. These emotions can either be used constructively or destructively. Oh yes, this was my lesson as a child dealing with a health issue.

I find very similar emotions well up during my interaction with the youth who attend our boot camps. Lots of them encounter sexual abuse by a close relative and don't share their struggles with a parent or guardian because of the fear of judgment and lack of trust. Most of the defining encounters that brought them sadness and grief happened to them as children.

When I encountered my loss of health, I was a child as well and I was met with so much judgment; other kids did not want to hang out with me. It wasn't much about what was said, but how I was ostracized.

My mom wouldn't take me to parties both to protect me and to avoid friends calling her to ask, "What's wrong with your child?" This was hard to deal with as a child, but it changed me in the process. When the environment where you dwell becomes hostile toward you, your first inclination is to run into your shell. What you cultivate in your shell gives you the capacity to build up yourself so that you can face the world in a new light when you eventually come out of your shell. With all that was happening around me due to my health condition, I cultivated faith in God in my shell. It gave me the strength to believe in myself and not depend on external validation to affirm my self-worth. When I was tired of solely relying on my medication for healing, I sought God by faith.

During this period, I was exposed to the performing arts in church. I wrote stage plays and performed them alongside other youth in church. I sang in the choir and I was very committed. These expressions were valid outlets for managing my emotions and drawing strength from others within my immediate creative community. It was therapeutic and healing.

This isn't often the case with a lot of young people. Sometimes their shells are empty or filled with negative energy that leads them to suicide, drugs, and the like. Due to the emptiness in their shell, they come out seeking validation from anyone who cares, such as gangs or illicit relationships.

This is why at Street Project Foundation, we have a circle of trust created where young people who are dealing with mental health issues can, through the arts, let go of their emotions with the support of a creative community. When they perform their stories and see the impact their stories have on an audience, they feel a sense of purpose that brings relief.

DEALING WITH THE LOSS OF A JOB

On my talk show, *Online with REO*, I had the opportunity to talk with a friend and sister from another mother, StephREDD. She is an identity, self-engineering, and communications coach. In my interview with her, we discussed dealing with loss (Ezenwa-Okoro, 2022).

Four months after starting a prestigious global job that she had testified about in a large church, she got fired. She doubted the very core of her identity when this happened. She doubted anyone who thought of her as a fantastic, certified human resource expert. This loss shook her Christian faith. It was a harsh and rude reality that brought her to the end of herself. The next option would have been despair, depression, and suicide. She told herself that suicide was not an option.

I then asked, "What should one do when they come to the end of themselves? You decided that suicide was not an option, but that isn't the case for many out there, so what should they do?" This is what she said:

Experiences differ. We don't respond from a place of knowledge but a place of programming. We have been programmed since we were born through an intentional engagement. Part of my programming was that I saw my mother say [that] "not on her watch will she see her children go hungry because of the loss of her husband." There is an unconscious programming of resilience. As such, it will take an intentional self-engagement to build the place of resilience because perspectives will differ due to differences of experience.

This is why I find the creative arts so instrumental to the unconscious reprogramming of our mindsets. This is because of its capacity to enable the youth to create an alternative universe of being and existing in the world. Play and performance gives them the tools they can use to create unique anchors for self-discovery, self-actualization, and mental health wellness.

One of the young people who attended our Creative Youth Boot Camp once asked, what makes the environment in the camp so different? Being in the camp made her feel secure but the moment she walked out the door of the camp into the real world, she was filled with trepidation because of past experiences that left her sleeping under bridges in the cold with nothing but raw pepper for food. She also mentioned her several failed attempts to commit suicide. Using her singing gift to express her uncertainty about life and venturing into upcycled art, which involved a lot of painting, cutting, remodeling, and repurposing of plastic and fabric waste, made her think of her future with more optimism. I told her the camp felt different because here, she had learned to use art to express herself and she now belonged to a creative community where she experienced love and support.

The relationship between the arts and mental health is well established in the field of art therapy, which applies arts-based techniques (like painting, dancing, and role play) as evidence-based interventions for mental health issues, such as anxiety and depression. There is also growing evidence that the arts can be used in non-therapy contexts for promoting mental health, such as using performing arts to learn about the core subject areas in schools or doing visual art with adults who are mentally well and want to sustain that sense of wellness. In other words...the arts can be used to build capacity for managing one's mental and emotional well-being (Martin, 2020).

I am interested in mental health wellness because it is a window for profound creative expression. As I work with young people, creating safe spaces for them to thrive is essential. Kids need an environment where they can honestly question things and build a circle of trust. A space where the youth choose to reflect, listen, and understand why people are the way they are and not judge them. One of the keywords is listening and understanding. When one can listen to other people without their internal noise, you can genuinely understand their pain and proffer a solution or provide support where needed. By so doing, we create a safe space for development.

GOOD COUNSEL

During one of the elections conducted for one of our creative youth boot camp cohorts, a young woman stood up to be elected alongside four other male contestants.

After the first round of elections, there was a clear winner for the cohort president and a tie between her and another contestant for the role of vice president. A young man flippantly made a statement, "Make una give am vice president; she be woman." He wanted me to compensate her for not winning the presidential election since she was the only woman.

She immediately took offense and instead of addressing the issue head-on with him, she quit. It was an emotionally charged decision. She was well within her right to be angry because she did not want to be handed over any privileges because of her gender but also because she was just as capable and suitable for the role. However, it became a teachable moment for everyone in the camp. She allowed the hurtful perspective of one person to affect a life-transforming opportunity to become a leader of her cohort.

When I engage with young people, I am always on the lookout for spontaneous teachable moments, and this was one moment I wouldn't let slide.

Several people have made decisions that have come back to haunt them. When they review their decisions, they realize it was made during a desperate position or an emotionally charged moment. An acquaintance of mine rushed into marriage because of the loss of a loved one. A couple of years later, the realization was that a mistake had been made primarily based on emotional trauma. Patience is needed in an emotionally charged environment; navigating through those emotions is a developmental exercise. It allows you to reflect both logically and emotionally at the same time.

"Never make a permanent decision about a temporary situation."

—T.D. JAKES

Decision-making is so critical to our existence on Earth. It can make us or break us. We cannot afford to allow our emotions to dictate how we assess a situation or challenge. Decisions shouldn't be rushed. We must acknowledge our emotions, but we should not make permanent decisions while experiencing them. We must pause and allow our emotions to take their full course. After which, we can engage our logical sense of reasoning. If you need to make hasty decisions due to the urgency of the circumstance, it is advisable to seek counsel from someone you trust.

The Bible states that,

> *"A nation falls through a lack of guidance, but victory comes through the counsel of many."*
>
> —PROVERBS 11:14 ISV

One of the critical decisions the youth would have to make borders around their career paths. Don't be hasty about making this decision regardless of the pressure from home to become a breadwinner because of the loss of a parent or sudden responsibility placed on you because of sudden grief. Explore, absorb, and enjoy the process of discovering all that is within you; performing arts is an incredible outlet to do just that. There's a famous quote by an American Trappist monk and writer,

> "Art enables us to find ourselves and lose ourselves simultaneously."
>
> —THOMAS MERTON

I find this saying very profound. As an artist, I believe that to be in touch with the novelty of our creative genius, we must empty our souls and spirits of vile emotions. Emotions that result from life's issues cause a bottleneck in the outpouring and flow of creativity. The performance of art is such a spiritual activity that it helps you get lost in a zone outside the physical. The intrigue of the arts is in finding your way when you're lost in it all. Finding your way is usually a point of reflection where your logical reasoning meshes with your emotions, and a breakthrough moment happens that sets you off on a creative expedition.

The loss of life, a job, or health are triggers that take one to the dark corners of life. However, your ability to reframe your narrative about the effect of that loss in your life will bring you out of that utter darkness. The loss and grief I experienced was a catalyst for building resilience in my life. It became the propelling force for my doing and being in life. Grief fuels various emotions, and I find that these emotions can be recycled through play and performance and serve as a critical tool for reflections that lead to making the right decisions.

According to Douglas Mitchell's Good Therapy blog post published in March 2012,

Expressive arts therapy encourages movement of the imagination that we may struggle with during our grieving process. Our art influences how we look at, unblock, wrestle with, and shed light on the need to distance and detach from our pain. When we dodge grief to avoid, deny, or block the inevitable pain, the arts invite the imagination of these stuck places to come to the surface in images, movement, color, and sound. Our art process releases the tension of grief, allowing it to expand and contract while providing a safe container in which this process can take place. When we create, we give ourselves permission to examine all that is happening within our griev-ing bodies.

For some children, engaging in creative arts such as drawing, clay modeling, and painting can have a tremendously posi-tive impact. By using arts and crafts as an emotional outlet, grieving children can begin to express their grief and open up about their thoughts and emotions with others (Crossroads Hospice Charitable Foundation, 2015).

I often tell my youth that the test of a novel piece of art is its ability to evoke any kind of emotion. Art shouldn't be indif-ferent. Art should speak. When we are aware of our grief and reframe it using the creative arts, we permit ourselves to be free. We speak truth to ourselves and the society around us, a revolutionary activity fueled by the developmental force of grief.

I was introduced to this performatory exercise by Cathy Salit, the chief organizer of the Global Play Brigade, a movement of performance activists who provide free play workshops during the pandemic and beyond for growth, development, and healing. She was my teacher at the East Side Institute, where I was introduced to the concept of social therapeutics and performance activism during a ten-month course organized by East Side Institute New York called International Class. My cohort was a class of twelve agents of change from the UK, US, Puerto Rico, Taiwan, Japan, Greece, and Nigeria. I was grieving a loved one, and no one in the group was aware because my smiley face covered up much of what I truly felt. This exercise helped me come to terms with the grief I was feeling for a loved one who died in Nigeria while I was in New York attending the training workshop.

With Cathy's support, I could reframe the grief I was feeling through the performance of a collaborative poem about how much my loved one meant to me.

PERFORMANCE OF A LIFETIME

1. Designate a "stage."
2. Tell the youth that they will have just sixty seconds to perform the events of their life using any creative medium: drama, music, dance, poetry, visual arts, etc. It could be a moment in their life or their entire life.
3. Make sure the observing group celebrates with vigor anyone performing on stage.
4. After the individual's sixty-second performance, recreate the scenario with one or two persons involved. This will require an imaginative mind. As the session curator, build on the first performance by adding another layer of direction to the performance, and often one or two more characters are added to the scene. This may be a humorous encore performance but in slow motion or fast forward. This direction makes the individual in question play with a story in their life from a different perspective.
5. When this is done, get others to perform until everyone in your group gets to go.

Note: Create space for your youth to decompress after the activity.

When I run this session, there's often catharsis. Sometimes one person's performance may trigger a certain emotion within the audience. Ensure there is an adult in the space to whom they can talk to. Make the room accommodating for people's vulnerability. I tell my youth that it's okay to cry regardless of your gender. Emotions were created for a reason and what's important is to create safe spaces for expression and healing.

Breathing exercises are perfect for decompressing. Here's one activity you could do with your youth:

- Relax your neck and shoulders.
- Keeping your mouth closed, inhale slowly through your nose for two counts.
- Pucker or purse your lips as though you were going to whistle.
- Exhale slowly by blowing air through your pursed lips for a count of four (Cronkelton, 2019).

Other things that can be done to decompress are squeezing an object, hugging tightly, and journaling. I use these tools for stabilizing emotions after a performance of a lifetime.

CHAPTER FOUR

SHINE YOUR LIGHT

Switch on the light.

The truth finder.

This is what performing art means to me. It is a unique kind of light that mirrors characters in society and the consequences of their actions on human existence.

Marianne Williamson's poem, titled "Our Deepest Fear," is one that we recite at the Creative Youth Boot Camp that Street Project Foundation organizes three to four times a year. We recite it so many times that before the four- to six-week boot camp or youth convenings elapse, participants of the program can recite it by heart. I am a big fan of this poem because it is a force of light that reveals the strengths and weaknesses of a human being and an affirmation of who we should be in the world. The line I often reflect on is the part about being frightened by our own light. It says, "it is our light, not our darkness that most frightens us" (Williamson, 1992).

I listened to Reverend Al Sharpton's message during George Floyd's memorial service on June 4, 2020, and I was moved by his analogy of cockroaches.

One thing I found out about roaches is that if you keep the light off, if you're in the dark, a roach will pull up to your dinner table and have a five-course meal. So, I learned that one of the ways to deal with roaches is if you cut the light on, I could run them roaches and track them down [...]. (Rev, 2020)

In this instance, Reverend Al Sharpton was referring to the faulty justice system that led to the death of George Floyd and many other victims of police brutality in the United States of America. My interpretation of his message was that it wasn't just a call for America to shine the light on the injustices in the country, but a call to the whole world to shine their light so that collectively we can track down and stop the "roaches," or in this case, the perpetrators causing mayhem in our world today.

In October 2020, the youth of Nigeria woke up from their slumber to protest against police brutality across the nation. It is critical to note that the penultimate nationwide protest in Nigeria occurred in 2012. It was called Occupy Nigeria. It was a protest in response to the removal of the fuel subsidy of the Federal Government of President Goodluck Ebele Jonathan. I joined this march, and proudly. Eight years later in 2020, following thought-provoking stories of young men and women who had been brutally mistreated by the Special Anti-Robbery Squad, popularly known as SARS, based on their looks and what they own, a nationwide protest march ensued. Youths were on social media, simultaneously clamoring for the end of SARS. The performance of this protest arrested the attention of not only the Federal Government of Nigeria but also the international community, which was enough to make it a priority issue.

The protest, which started as a hashtag in 2017, gained ground in October 2020. It is my personal opinion that based on the principle of the cultivation theory I mentioned in Chapter One, the #BlackLivesMatter movement, which had gone global, having a similar premise of police brutality, influenced the Nigerian youth to a large extent. Like their counterparts in the United States, they were inspired to fight for justice for their brothers and sisters who had been unlawfully killed and maimed. Through social media, a nationwide protest was organized. Food and water were provided for people at protest grounds. The organizing was very commendable. The protest lasted for two weeks.

Protesting on the streets for a cause you believe in is a kind of performance. Like William Shakespeare would say,

> "All the world's a stage, and all the men and women merely players."

> —AS YOU LIKE IT, SHAKESPEARE

It requires that we take on a specific type of confident, stern, and articulate personae. One takes on an animated character, holding placards, screaming at the top of your lungs, and riling the crowd to keep their energy levels up for the long haul. This live performance inspired by a need for change is developmental for our society and for building youth leadership. In this chapter, we will be exploring how the performing arts can become a typification of light that enables individuals and organizations to come to terms with the truth about themselves and serve as a stimulus for confidence and leadership building.

Light is such an essential force that even the Bible references the importance of "light" in fixing the world.

In the beginning, God created the heaven and the earth. And the earth was without form, and void; and darkness was upon the face of the deep. And the Spirit of God moved upon the face of the waters.

And God said, Let there be light: and there was light.

GENESIS 1:1-3 (KJV)

After the darkness, voidness, and lack of form on Earth were expressed, God's next creation was light, and then God began to *create* all the things the world needed. To fix anything sustainably in life, you must first identify the problem. Not only was the earth destroyed, but there was also gross darkness. It was important for the spirit of God to assess the situation, so He called forth light.

THE MAGIC BULLET

When I started in the development sector during my youth corp year, one of the first trainings I attended was called Logical Framework. The key to this framework is being able to ask "why?" This helps dig for the cause of a problem. If you can understand the problem, you can then plan for change.

In advertising, when a client sends a brief to launch a brand, the strategy department embarks on research to understand the context where the brand wants to be launched. They also embark on a target audience profiling, a competitive analysis to understand the market, and a deep dive into the brand's unique offerings. The essence of all this research is to find a "magic bullet" that will shot to the top of the market—hit the bulls eye and unlock the sale of that brand every time.

The magic bullet is the insight of an undeniable truth about the consumers as it relates to the brand's category. This insight inspires the creative development of print, television, radio, and social media advertising that can persuade the target audience to purchase the brand.

Why does "our light frighten us" when it gives us the foresight to see what is stopping our greatness and the insight that helps us create solutions? The entrance of light illuminates our minds to see the stumbling blocks that our perceptions, doctrines, and faulty cultural and religious practices have developed. There is a saying that goes, "A problem well defined is a problem half solved," and to define a problem, we must shine our light on the cause.

I was particularly moved by Luvvie Ajayi Jones's TED talk, where she introduces herself as a "professional troublemaker" (Jones, 2017). Luvvie Ajayi Jones is a Nigerian American two-time New York Times bestselling author, speaker, and podcaster. Her life's mission is to speak up and critique issues that people know about and are affected by but find hard to talk about. This is how she chooses to affect change in her world by calling the attention of those in power to fix the issues that affect our world at large.

Have you ever looked into the eyes of a person in authority or position of power and spoken an unpalatable truth to them? Two things can happen. You get cut off from their circle immediately and get some bad press, or they are moved by your honesty and ask you more questions to figure out how they can perform better. Either way, it is a challenging position to be in. Speaking the truth to power requires a level of confidence and fearlessness.

TRUTH IS LIGHT

My late paternal grandfather was conferred with a chieftaincy title called, in Esan, *Otemuata,* or one who speaks the truth. This title was given to him because he was known to be very bold, and anywhere in the community, he was called upon to judge because he was never afraid to speak the truth. People didn't like him for being forthright, even within his family. This title was also passed on to my late father, who followed in his footsteps, and I can tell you firsthand that speaking the truth to power isn't easy, but it is necessary. My late father, before his passing, was an elder in the church, which meant he had to sit in after church services to deliberate on issues regarding the church's growth.

There were many times he would take a stance that did not align favorably with the lead pastor's position but as long as his position was one of truth, he never backed down. There was one instance where the lead pastor had to visit him at home to make peace after a heated disagreement. The pastor's visitation was a gesture that reflected his respect for my father's position on the matter. To date, my late father remains a very respected figure, but it came at a price that only truth can reveal.

Luvvie in her TED talk speaks about the domino effect: one domino has to fall for others to follow. Isn't it interesting that it took one person to start the #MeToo movement, the #BlackLivesMatter movement, or #EndSARS? Still, these movements spiraled on social media and led to large national protests. When these movements gather momentum, those in power have no choice but to respond. This is because by speaking up, we illuminate our world so those in authority cannot deny the need to take action and fix the mess.

During a conversation with my husband, Ezenwa Okoro, who hails from eastern Nigeria, he shared this adage with me in Igbo, *"Onye ji onyeya n' ala ji onweye."* In explaining this adage, he referenced a wrestling match. When a wrestler pins his opponent down, it is difficult for the opponent to stand up and continue the fight. So, imagine that you are wrestling with yourself, and the opponent pinning you down is yourself; how can you get up? One of the hardest truths to tell is the truth to self.

I find that when we are not truthful with ourselves, it feels like a dark cloud limiting us from becoming all that we can attain here on Earth. It's so easy to cast aspersions on others, but when those same aspersions are thrown at us, it isn't easy to stand it. This is where I find the concept of play and performance helpful. It is easier to open up through play than do it yourself. Play and performance require the presence of community, like someone in your circle of trust to perform a conversation, for instance.

One of such illuminating moments was when I was conversing with a life coach and friend about my tendency to place my career ahead of family. It all started with a simple gesture of closing my eyes to envision my future and defining what success looked like when I was old and frail. I shocked myself after the exercise because all I could imagine was my work with young people and global influence.

When I opened my eyes to reflect, I realized that, for once, I did not mention family. I was concerned about my lack of central focus on family: that was the truth, no excuses. I took ownership of what I considered a flaw in my priorities, and I have since reframed what success means to me with a central focus on family. This could only be possible with illuminating performance of conversations. The intriguing thing was I didn't need to be told by my friend about the insight I drew from the process of the exercise; I figured it out myself.

Street Project Foundation's award-winning innovative intervention tool for youth engagement called reflection sessions uses this method quite well. We find it compelling because it isn't prescriptive, the youth figure out the truth about themselves during a performance, and upon reflection, they decide their next step of action. This is because the power of choice and the decision to change lies in the youth. They realize that the ability to make sound decisions lies within them. This develops their confidence in decision-making, and I find this approach very effective. By engaging with weighty subjects such as rape, poverty, family challenges, corruption, school issues, and career choices through simple, playful exercises, they begin to self-reflect on their lives. Like a domino, others who have faced similar circumstances share their stories, and steps are taken to address their past issues. This stirs up conversations that help our youth find a shoulder to lean on for emotional support.

When we can successfully speak up about our truth, it is easier to speak truth to others. One of the most critical tasks for youth workers is the ability to build the confidence level of the youth who struggle to speak up boldly. During my sessions on public speaking at the Creative Youth Boot Camp, I use one of the scenes in a stage play written and directed by Felix Okolo titled *Mekunu Melody* (Ogunbiyi, 2016). This is a play that I got the chance to perform with known names in the film and television industry in Nigeria, such as Joke Silva, Yinka Davies, and the late Funsho Alabi. At age eighteen, I had to play the role of a fifty-year-old woman, who was the first lady to the community leader; it was a rally scene, and I had to say this line: "My people, we need a change of leadership, oracle or no oracle."

This line stuck with me because it helped me find my voice. It was a significant line for the transition of the play, but I found it challenging to deliver in the way the director wanted me to depict the character. Don't forget that I was just a teenager trying so hard to become a woman in her fifties. At that moment, I needed a coach, and the director realized this and asked Aunty Joke to work with me privately. I had no repository of experiential knowledge about how a fifty-year-old woman should act, so Aunty Joke chose to teach me how to inflect my voice like a Martin Luther King Jr. addressing the civil rights movement.

After a couple of minutes with her, I got back on stage. When we got to the rally scene where the lines were to be recited, I channeled my inner Martin Luther King; everyone was shocked, including the director, about my sudden transformation on stage. I did it! The opportunity to perform with mentors like Aunty Joke on stage aided my development in public speaking.

When I coach the youth on public speaking, I use the same lines from the play to boost their confidence and exercise their vocal tones. I identify the youth with confidence issues and make them stand on a raised platform to stand taller than the audience in front of them. I get them to recite the lines from *Mekunu Melody*, and when they seem to catch the drift of the exercise, I ask them to talk about themselves with the same vigor and vibrancy.

The youth perform what they are until they can perform whom they are becoming.

Performing what you are is not casting a light on what it feels like to be in someone else's shoes. In hindsight, the empathy experienced in trying to fit into someone else's character makes you humble enough to reflect on how you relate to nature and develop meaningful interaction with that character. This makes you more vulnerable, sincere, and honest about the experience of the performance of the character. In like manner, this reflection of characters is an approach that can be used for self-reflection of your thoughts and actions.

SELF-REFLECTION ON LIGHT

I better understand the scripture on the creation of the first light, the light created before the sun, moon, and stars. That light is the "truth" about the actual state of affairs of the earth, which triggers the god in us to create and fix what isn't functioning correctly. This is why I am so in love with the work of development because by identifying problems, we can conceptualize and create solutions that can make the world a better place to live in, free of the roaches that Reverend Al Sharpton talks about in his speech that I referred to earlier in this chapter.

What about the thought of standing out, being different, or being the lone voice in the crowd makes us so afraid of shining our light? Why do we feel like impostors when a responsibility we perceive to be higher than our capabilities is given to us? We must realize that like Marrianne Williamson's poem alludes, we are powerful because of the innate God-given talents that are resident in our beings. By applying performing arts principles and innovations like improvisation, drama, music, spoken word, and poetry for expression, we can play with the idea of what we want to become until we are whom we want to be. It is through the consistent exposure to the practice of performance that we can build confidence enough, such that we don't think of ourselves as impostors but as co-creators in the world.

The construct of social therapeutics recognizes that people are social beings, performers, improvisers, and revolutionaries. Upon understanding who we are, we will learn that the world is what it is because of us. A fellow Global Play Brigadier, Jeff Gordon, once shared a quote that has stuck with me. He said, "We cannot turn off the darkness; we can only turn on the light." Darkness already exists in the world; it is left for us to turn on our lights so that the world will be illuminated with goodness.

A brilliant mind is an enlightened mind, and an enlightened mind needs no permission to shine. When you shine your light, you unconsciously permit other people to shine their lights also. Grooming young leaders requires intentionally creating an environment where they can perform their truth through an immersive storytelling process. It positions them in a vulnerable place to co-create stories that can, in turn, serve as a mirror for society. When the youth perform their truth, they build the confidence needed to transform their societies. They become unafraid of their own truth and unafraid to speak truth to power with an unrelenting pursuit for change. The more change agents we can raise in our societies, the more we increase the intensity of light that our nations can radiate unto other countries.

MIRRORING EXERCISE

1. Separate the youth into pairs.
2. Tell them to face their partner and look into their eyes for ninety seconds.
3. After ninety seconds, while still looking into each other's eyes, tell them to imitate their partner's movement. This activity can go on for another sixty seconds.

4. Once sixty seconds is over, they can stop. Ask what they saw in their partner's eyes.

5. You can ask them to write a poem, song, or perform a dance piece that reflects what they saw in their partner's eyes.

6. Build conversations with the performances they showcase or stories they share.

CHAPTER FIVE

PLAY

—

Let us play!

Jangolova!

This word is a Nigerian colloquial reference to the swings we played on as kids.

I attended St. Jude's nursery and primary school in Festac Town and my fondest memory as a child was on the playground. The playground was what demarcated the primary school from the nursery school. It was a sea of sand divided into two parts by a pavement that served as a walkway from the nursery school to the primary school. We had swings, slides, see-saws, a badminton court, and a revolving rollercoaster.

With all of these fun activities in the playground, we still found time out of our break to play pretend. Role-playing meant we didn't play alone. We learned to call other children like ourselves to join us and we made space for them within the construct of our play. The beauty of child's play is that it is open-ended and could change no matter the circumstance. The fact that the performance started with me playing

Mommy didn't mean I had to be Mommy from beginning to end. The characters evolved for no reason at all.

Having an intact childhood is such a blessing and I don't take it for granted. This is because poverty has robbed many of a proper childhood. When children are robbed of play, their early childhood development, which is essential to life, is affected. In this chapter, we will be exploring the role of play within the context of a poverty-stricken society.

The number of people living in extreme poverty is on the rise in sub-Saharan Africa. Forecasts indicate that by 2030, nearly nine in ten extremely poor people will live in sub-Saharan Africa (Schoch and Christoph, 2020).

Latest estimates show there are 86.6 million children in child labor in sub-Saharan Africa, which is more than in the rest of the world combined, and the vast majority, four out of every five children, are engaged in child labour within the agriculture sector (FAO, 2021).

As a result of the extreme poverty in the global south like Nigeria, children are not allowed to be children. As soon as a child is able to walk and comprehend language, they quickly are put on the streets to sell commodity items like water, local snacks, boiled groundnuts, and a variety of other things. The limited resources at home force parents to expand their streams of income by leaning on child labor. Some parents give out their children as house help to well-to-do families. If the child is fortunate, they are sent to school in exchange for their labor. For some, it is a hellish experience; they receive no education and no opportunity to play. Rather, they experience abuse that causes them a lifetime of trauma.

According to a *VOA* report of May 2022 by France-Presse UNICEF states that "18.5 million Nigerian children are out of school." Sixty percent of this number are girls. UNICEF has warned of an increase in reported cases of child marriage and early pregnancy.

Can you imagine how many adults today in sub-Saharan Africa alone have been robbed of their childhood because of poverty? There are many in the continent of Africa who did not play sufficiently as children. When children are robbed of play, nations are robbed of education, artistry, and character development.

Working as a developmentalist in the youth space, I am continuously exposed to the stories of the youth who lost their childhood to poverty. The death of parents, the failure of relatives to love and care for their wards, early child marriage, child abuse, and teenage pregnancies all rob kids of their right to be kids. There are traumatic incidences where eleven-year-olds become the breadwinners and caretakers of their siblings due to poverty. Seven-year-olds hawk food items to help put food on the table alongside their parents.

When poverty continues to prevail in a country like Nigeria where over seventy million people live in extreme poverty, representing 33 percent of the nation's population, and the population has a median age of 18.1 years, it is the children of the nation that are starved of holistic development, and the future of the nation is jeopardized (Oluwole, 2022, Worldmeter, 2022).

We are living at a time of an unprecedented loss of play among people of all ages. Today's children have fewer opportunities for free play than previous generations and adults are working more, playing less, and plagued by increased stress. The loss of play—and of opportunities for playfully engaging with the world—is particularly pronounced in poor communities. In many instances, the opportunity to engage in pointless play has become a luxury, especially for children who, in and out of school, are drilled and "remediated" rather than related to as playful, creative, improvisational learners (East Side Institute, 2021).

Have you ever wondered why it might be hard for some kids living in a deprived community in Nigeria to dream about spaceships landing on planet Mars or managing the traffic of drones? When there's no food in the belly, how does a child or adult think of playing?

This is why when we organize boot camps at Street Project Foundation, we ensure participants are well fed in the morning and afternoon. This way, when we introduce the concept of play in the space, they are very receptive and engage in many pointless activities without question. The point, however, is that it is through these activities that they learn to co-create together with an open mind devoid of concerns about their basic needs like food, water, and transportation.

The year 2020 was when the word "palliatives" became a part of my vocabulary due to the COVID-19 pandemic. In my first opinion editorial titled "Is a new world being created?" I referenced the sudden welfare system that emerged during the compulsory lockdown period that lasted for four months in Nigeria. Here's an excerpt of what I wrote:

I am particularly moved by the character development that I see among everyday people, who are, in Alicia Keys words, "the underdog." Seeing a country like Nigeria talk about palliatives and welfare, I consider it a good character development for my country. State governments making efforts to provide food for the vulnerable is a good development but truth be told, it shouldn't take a pandemic to let our leaders know that there is hunger in the land. So, how do we build on these things? How do we ensure that this development is not a flash in the pan?

When I thought that our leaders were becoming humane, the #EndSARS movement happened. Then, the so-called "hoodlums," who hijacked the protests after the horrific treatment of protesters at the Lekki toll gate by law enforcement agents, located storehouses where bags upon bags of foodstuff that should have been distributed as palliatives to citizens were kept. It took a disruption in the state through the hijack of the #EndSARS protest for the people of Nigeria to find out about food allocation that was rightfully theirs locked up in a location. That disruption broke us free from doing the same thing and expecting a different result. It is time to create alternative ways by which we can change the poverty in the African continent. We don't need another world leader like the United States' forty-fifth president to call us a "shit-hole nation" for us to sit up and create a future where our children can play and develop (Haltiwanger, 2018).

COMMUNITY-LED INTERVENTIONS

Many years ago in New York, the All-Stars Project was founded by Lenora Fulani and Fred Newman. The goal was to transform the lives of youth in poor communities. They discovered that the inner-city youth wanted to dance, sing, act, recite poems, perform, and engage in many creative endeavors and so the programs of the All-Stars were fashioned. Using techniques of grassroots organizing and community building, funds were raised through donations from random people on the streets of New York. The lesson here for poor communities across the African continent is this: We cannot continue to wait for donations, contributions, and grants from the Western world.

We need to commit at community levels to liberate ourselves. We must learn to organize to liberate ourselves from poverty. We cannot depend on our governments and international communities. In order to liberate our communities and alleviate poverty, we must invest in the arts on an individual level, fundraise, and tell others about why the youth and the arts are so important.

Rose Maruru, co-founder and CEO of EPIC-Africa, an organization that works to increase the impact of philanthropy in Africa, says when international NGOs serve as intermediaries, African CSOs are reduced to "foot soldiers."

"They have no say in the issues or solutions that get prioritized, even when they know better," she tells Quartz. "It means that their work is donor-driven rather than community-led." In this model, she adds, the relationship between African and international CSOs are rarely partnerships to co-create solutions but contractor-sub-contractor relation-ships where the African CSOs are contracted to deliver spe-cific outputs (Mureithi, 2021).

One example of a community-led resource model in the global south is an organization in India called Mitti Cafe. Mitti Cafe is a chain of cafes that provide training and employment to adults with physical and intellectual dis-abilities. The cafes are sustained by the patronage of people within the communities. In the last four years of its existence, they have served over five million meals. They currently have sixteen cafes, including within institutions such as the banks, hospitals, consultancy firms, and more. Their model of intervention creates awareness about disability rights and inclusion.

Maruru says African CSOs should reduce their depen-dence on one funding source—be it local or foreign—to strengthen their financial sustainability. "Growing their own assets, and leveraging local resources, could be a way to build the foundation for financial sustainability so that if all external funding were to dry up, a CSO would not have to shut down."

This rings true for development organizations in the creative sector. We need to deploy strategies for reducing dependence on one funding source. To successfully make this a reality, we must galvanize a community that values the creative arts, especially in the global south where govern-ment funding for the creative and culture industry is almost nonexistent. The community needs to take ownership, and one way we can begin to cultivate the kind of community that will take ownership of development initiatives using the creative arts is by creating an ecosystem where it's normal for adults and children alike to embrace the concept of play.

For example, we can play with the concept of building a community, conscious of inclusion like the founder of Mitti Cafe, Alina Alam.

What is very important in any initiative that you take up is that the community would have to own it. Mitti Cafe is not Mitti Cafe because of me; I am irrelevant. Right from the local electrician who decided to repair our secondhand fridge for free, to the local printer who translated the vacancy pamphlets for me and did not charge me a penny, to the vegetable vendors who gave out this vase basket for free, everything is for free. The community has owned this initiative and, by the way, if you don't have money, you become very creative. So initially when we started, the café, it was completely designed by our people with disabilities [...] with the help of the community [...]. Any initiative for it to be sustainable has to be community-driven and that is a nonnegotiable (TEDx Talks, 2020).

PLAYFULNESS

The beautiful thing about being childlike is one's openness to play. It frees up the mind of all the weight that comes with living life. I remember vividly when I worked for an advertising agency as a copywriter, constantly brainstorming ideas with my art director to sell brand offerings, we often hit a brick wall in the process, or a block where ideas don't flow. When this happens, we play: We talk about things unrelated to the job, joke about things, and engage in anything that will take the pressure off work. In short, we engaged in very pointless activities, and then boom, we magically landed on a point of meaningful creation. Someone says something or does something that stimulates a round of creative splurge and we get back to the groove of creating compelling stories again. Edutopia corroborates this point in their article about eleven ways to help students to overcome creative blocks.

"Play is key to liberating your ideas and removing inhibitions to your creativity. Unfortunately, we have to relearn methods of playfulness that allow younger children to quickly learn a new skill. Toying around with questions, ideas, nonsensical words, or a relevant object is a great way for students to loosen up and open up their ideas."

—STACEY GOODMAN, ARTIST AND EDUCATOR
FROM OAKLAND, CALIFORNIA

Play lends itself to imagination. During an interview with Alex Sutherland, a developmentalist from South Africa who runs a project called Imagine Otherwise, she stated, "to imagine is an act of hope."

I can relate to that quote in many ways because creating new pathways in one's mind is a result of a vision for an alternative way of living. This is why I'm in love with the creative arts and the possibilities it provides because when you can think of it, you can have it.

There's a story in the Bible that lends itself to the power of imagination and it is the story about the Tower of Babel. According to Genesis, the Babylonians wanted to make a name for themselves by building a mighty city and a tower with its top in the heavens. The Bible states that God saw what the children of men built and said:

> "The people is one, and they
> have one language; and this
> they have imagined to do."

—GENESIS 11:6 (KJV)

This presupposes that whatever a person imagines doing is as good as done because the process of creation starts in the mind and play is a process of training one's mind to create. The process of imagination is so powerful that the Bible scripture states that the Babylonians were so united in their thought that God had to confound their language. This is because if they had continued with their united thoughts, they would have accomplished their desire.

> "Go to, let us go down, and there
> confound their language, that they may
> not understand one another's speech."

—GENESIS 11:7 (KJV)

When we engage in play, we are exercising our creative muscles and, more than ever before, we need to imagine, not just as an act of hope but as an act of necessity in a world that is constantly changing as a result of new technologies, climate change, wars, and bad governance.

Play isn't just for children: it's for everyone, everywhere. In the Yoruba language, play is translated as *"sere,"* or a performance that requires one to act as someone other than themselves. It is also considered an activity associated with children and so adults have no business engaging in these activities. This is the kind of thinking about play that must be changed. Adults need to play as much as children do.

Many people think playtime is reserved for children. As a result, it's not always something that grown-ups intentionally schedule into their daily routines. But experts note that there are many benefits of play—and for people of all ages. Peter Gray, a research professor of psychology and neuroscience at Boston College, studies play for a living. He says that some of the many benefits of making time for playing include a reduction in stress and anxiety, increased social bonding, an instant mood boost, and a way to foster creativity and problem solving (Pajer, 2021).

With all that's happening in the world today, we hardly engage in play. You may even ask, what is there to play about? My answer to that is everything. The act of playing helps us stay sane in an insane world. It helps us imagine a world that is different; it also helps us interact with the challenges faced by people in the world when we play with serious issues in ways that are satirical.

At the start of the COVID-19 pandemic, Cathy R. Salit, the author of *Performance Breakthrough: A Radical Approach to Success at Work*, began organizing performance activists from all over the world with the goal to create free play workshops on Zoom and WhatsApp at the time the world was on lockdown. Truth be told, the goal wasn't that clear-cut from the beginning because we played our way to creating what the goal is becoming and I know this because I am a founding member of this revolutionary movement. When I asked Cathy about the process of developing the movement, she answered by saying, "What something is, is not knowable when you're in the middle of it."

I found that response profound. I find that play makes us open to the concept of not knowing what something is and comfortable with the process of creating what it is becoming (Salit, 2016).

At the Global Play Brigade, people play with their emotions in a community that is nonjudgmental and supportive of everyone else. As the movement evolved, it was also important to reach out to those on the frontline of the battle against the COVID-19 pandemic and people around the world who do not have access to platforms like Zoom due to the lack of infrastructure in their communities to access the world through seamless internet connections. I was glad to be one of those in the brigade that championed the revolutionary use of the WhatsApp platform, which has become a formidable tool used to run emotional support sessions for youth all over the world.

My dear friend and fellow Brigadier, Aurelie Harp, founder of Womanity Play and Womanity Project, and I teamed up to create a play activity called "Creating Together Here and Now." Thanks to technology, we tag teamed and developed a one-hour thirty minutes program to engage youth on WhatsApp. We used video, text, gifs, static pictures, and prompts to engage the youth on WhatsApp who signed up for the program.

The pilot edition was done with the youth from Nigeria and it was well-received. Following lessons learned from the pilot of the program, we opened it up to the Global Play Brigade community. Some of the play sessions we engaged in were, for instance, taking a selfie of yourself here and now and introducing yourself, or taking a picture of an object around you and posting it. We also had conversations in emojis and we sometimes tried to deduce what the emoji sentences meant. One activity I also loved when we played on WhatsApp is getting the youth from across the world to teach us a dance style by recording themselves dancing. We eventually rounded up the sessions by asking the youth to create a performance of their time during the play session on WhatsApp. We encouraged them to work in teams of twos or threes and post on the platform the following day. This is because play breeds creativity and brings people together. It's always amazing to watch the creative videos that the youth create as a result of this playful engagement on WhatsApp.

What we created on WhatsApp has evolved since Aurelie and I created this developmental play activity. Our fellow Brigadier, Jennifer Bullock, a social therapist based in Philadelphia, USA, has since embraced the use of WhatsApp to reach the underserved in the world through play. She provides, along with other Brigadiers, teen spaces and emotional support sessions as one of Global Play Brigade's workshop offerings.

More than ever before, the global south needs to create an ecosystem where play can thrive. Play helps us build community by blurring the lines that divide us as a people. Play is a revolutionary tool for development. The global south needs development and as such play must be prioritized at the grassroots level and corporate level. We need to stop the cycle of the children of today becoming adults who lost their childhood due to the adverse effects of poverty. Play is developmental and helps us rise above the limitations that poverty of the mind and poverty of resources may bring because it is a stimulus for creativity and innovation.

One of the coolest play activists I know is Marian Rich, a comic educator, performance activist, and play revolutionary based in New York City. For over thirty years she's supported people in unleashing their creativity and playfulness. A lot of the play activities I run in our creative boot camps at Street Project Foundation, I learned from her. One thing I love about her playfulness is the use of improvisation to get adults engaged in play. The first rules of improv are: Always make your partner look good, and "yes-and" (Rich, 2022).

1. INTRODUCTIONS
- Form a circle.
- Tell your youth to introduce themselves and the emotion they feel at that moment with a facial expression or body movement.
- After each introduction, the entire group must repeat the motion and reintroduce the person.
- What is important is that everyone mirrors each other's movement after they make their introductions.

2. COUNT TO SILLINESS
- Break up into pairs.
- Get each pair to count from one to five.
- After that is done, each person replaces each number with an action and a sound that they can perform together in synchronicity.

- They do this until numbers one to five are replaced with action and sound and performing with synchronicity and never losing eye contact in the process to keep the connection going.
- After this is done, three pairs come on stage to perform together but this time they stand in a line and perform in synchronicity.
- In the process they are prompted to perform slowly, fast, angrily, like old people, etc. This way, they get to perform a variety of emotions.

3. I AM A TREE

This helps the group create a tableau vivant: a silent and motionless group of people arranged to represent a scene or incident.

- Person One starts a story. In this example, we will use, "I am a tree." Person One form the posture of a tree and freeze.
- Person Two adds themself to the story. An example would be, "I am a squirrel moving under the tree." They form the posture of a squirrel and freeze.
- Each player gets the opportunity to describe what they are and place themselves in the scene.

One important thing to do after every play session is the opportunity to sit down and reflect on the activity. Get your youth to talk about the process, and how it made them feel, act, or think. Some philosophical conversations may begin to happen. You might ask yourself, "But we just played together?" Well, it isn't "just" play: it is development in motion.

CHAPTER SIX

COMMUNITY ORGANIZING

I love to move people and I love to move with them.

Being involved in an organized march of a large crowd of people all in agreement to pursue a cause moves me. I always wondered, however, why some advocacy marches in other parts of the world seemed more compelling because of their numbers compared to Nigeria, where numerous civil society organizations organize marches on Gender-Based Violence for instance, or their displeasure with a bill passed at the house of representatives or senate. The only exception was the "Enough is Enough" protest, also called Occupy Nigeria Movement, during which I proudly held my placard and marched alongside other Nigerian citizens to speak up for what we believed in.

The Occupy Nigeria Protests were a collective rejection of the Nigerian Government's sudden increase of Premium Motor Spirits (PMS) from ₦65 to ₦140 (Ebunike, 2015). The cost of petrol increased astronomically and this caused citizens of Nigeria to march in the streets.

In January 2012, that mass movement put the bloated Nigerian government in the crosshairs. It's believed to be Nigeria's biggest ever national mass protest. Apart from its sheer size, the movement managed to endure for days and weeks. And, in some ways, it set some impressive, unthinkable marks. For instance, some considered it unimaginable that Nigerians (often portrayed as too "happy," too timid and cowardly, or too polarized along ethno-religious lines) would unite behind a common cause. Also, it was unthinkable that a mass uprising would start from the nation's capital of Abuja, considered a fortress of the ruling interests (Sowore, 2013).

The march was a sign of dissatisfaction with the government's announcement to remove fuel subsidies thereby increasing fuel prices. In Nigeria, oil and gas are still significant drivers of the economy.

President Goodluck Jonathan's New Year's decision to remove a fuel subsidy—an act that doubled the price of fuel for Nigerians overnight—catapulted the movement, which has dubbed itself Occupy Nigeria. "Really from our perspective it was just a trigger," said Adamolekun of the end of the fuel subsidy. "Nigerians have been very quiet for so long. The corruption in the system is known at home and abroad. Lack of infrastructure, rising costs of goods and services" (Shryock, 2012).

An increase in any petroleum commodity affects the cost of doing business and that cost is passed on to the common man on the streets whose source of livelihood is based on what he or she earns per day. The cost is also passed on to the working class who struggle monthly to make ends meet to pay for transportation, food, shelter, and electricity. This is reiterated in a report by *The Guardian* on the increased cost of doing business by an average citizen as a result of the fuel hike.

Bisola Edun's electricity generator sits outside her small Lagos fashion shop and factory, noisily churning out heat and fumes for five hours every day. It is just one of an estimated 160m such machines across Nigeria—roughly one per person in Africa's top oil economy. Guzzling $1,200 (£780) worth of diesel each month, Edun's generator is an unavoidable expense in a country that produces only forty watts of power for each inhabitant—enough to run a single vacuum cleaner among twenty-five citizens. "It seems normal to us but looking at the amount I spend every year on the generator alone, I just think Jesus Lord! If I could spend that amount on stock I'd be in a very good place," she said (Mark, 2012).

The outcome of the Occupy Nigeria protest is one I was not happy with because of how disappointed I was with the negotiations by the leaders of the Labor Union. They compromised and shifted their position on the people's demand from the government.

For a moment, many Nigerians hoped that the "Occupy" movement would transition into the first sub-Saharan African Spring (or Harmattan). A year later, the conclusion is sobering. It is clear that "Occupy Nigeria" failed to metamorphose into a genuine, sustained mass movement. The central labor unions that were initially trusted to lead the movement capitulated quickly under the weight of accusations that they were conniving to overthrow the government (Sowore, 2013).

Could this be a reason why some of our protest marches are not compelling enough? Could it be as a result of the distrust for people we refer to as leaders of the people but who are really servants of their own selfish interests?

I felt close to the #EndSARS protests mostly because I had a good number of Street Project Youth Ambassadors on the streets marching. For a lot of them, it was their first time being a part of a protest march. A movement that had the capacity to change the status quo of police brutality in the country. Like every protest before it in Nigeria, we didn't get what we wanted, but we put a spotlight on the issue, which in itself is a movement of the needle on this social justice issue. The organizing and impact of the protest were effective enough to draw the attention of the international media, which isn't always the case.

Adejumo Kabir, in a *Premium Times* publication of November 17, 2020, categorically stated ten reasons why the #EndSARS protest attracted global attention. Some of the reasons cited were as follows: a unified agenda, the use of social media, the economic effect, the persistence of the protesters, the absence of a formal leadership structure, that it was devoid of partisan politics, President Buhari's long silence, high unemployment and poverty rate, coordination and logistics, and support from Nigerians in diaspora.

It was labeled a protest without any leader, but I beg to differ; even if there wasn't a proclaimed leader of the protests, there were people who took the lead in different clusters. The advantage of having multiple leaders however was the fact that when the leaders' resilience waned, it did not stop the protest. Other servant leaders continued from where they stopped. According to *Premium Times*:

Ordinarily, in the history of Nigerians, leaders of struggles meet with the authorities and after discussions, most times, they usually reach concessions that end such protests. In the case of #EndSARS protests, nobody nor group had the monopoly of power to ask protesters to stop demanding. When musician, Naira Marley, said he was no longer leading the protests, many Nigerians still went to the streets (Kabir, 2020).

SCHOOL POLITICS

In the year 1999, I joined student politics. I actively participated in politics on a departmental and faculty level.

I served as secretary-general of the Creative Arts Student Association (CASA). During my tenure, we led a protest march to the dean of student affairs office because of the lack of free campus hostel accommodations allocated to the Department of Creative Arts.

In addition, we demanded that the Theatre for the Faculty of Arts be handed over to the Creative Arts Department. This theatre facility was used by every department in the faculty arts for lectures. This meant that the creative arts students had no designated theatre space for dance and drama rehearsals. The Creative Arts Department was the youngest department in the faculty of arts at the time. It was formally referred to as the center for cultural studies. Being a young department, students of the creative arts did not enjoy the benefits that students from other departments enjoyed.

Working closely with the president of the association, Otun Rasheed, we mobilized all the students of the department of Creative Arts. We were clear about our demands. We designed placards and had our protest songs ready. We also had media coverage. On the day of our protest, we moved in mass marching to the Dean of Student Affairs office singing and chanting. I became a different person performing my anger and dissatisfaction. The goal during the march was to get everyone energized and railed up in unity so that our voices will be heard. We chanted "Greatest Casaites!" and "Great!" in a call-and-response fashion.

This chant created an environment that allowed the President to address everyone and motivate them to fight for their rights. Having a motivating speech is so important. During a protest, we often perform as improvisers, building on each other's creative articulation of the problem and desired solution.

It was an impactful march, enough for the local news to feature it as a story on television. I remember my choirmaster in church reprimanded me and wondered why I was screaming at the top of my voice with a fist in the air for the world to see as he had seen the protest on television. It was worth it because we got hostel accommodations allocated to several students of Creative Arts afterward. We didn't get the Arts Theatre, but we got a room in the faculty of arts building designated for music classes. Our protest was the start of other organizing and lobbying for what we wanted. While we made our demands, the head of the department and his team played their own role.

We didn't get all we wanted in 1999 but I returned to the university ten years after, and the department now has a huge structure built for them including a theatre. In many ways, this is what we hope for when people gather to fight for a cause. It might not happen in their time but what is important is the power of movements to trigger the fire. When you have supporters fanning the flame through creative activities on the street, social media, the press, and proper negotiations with experienced and influential people championing the discussions, we can indeed move the needle on social justice issues we care about.

NOT TOO YOUNG TO BE LEADERS

When I gained admission to study Creative Arts at the University of Lagos, I was the second youngest in the pioneer set of the department. There were about one hundred of us who eventually majored in Theatre Arts, Music, or Visual Arts. A lot of my coursemates were older than me by four years and above. I was sixteen years old, my late father called me "undergraduate *Kekere*," meaning "very young undergraduate" in Yoruba.

Living with brothers and sisters older than I was, by four years and more, prepared me for my time at the university. Age was nothing but a number. We were all there to get a degree and I was set to develop myself further. I want to believe I had shown a level of maturity at a young age, enough for me to have had people in my corner vying for me to become a leader in the department. One thing I certainly knew I was good at was getting things done.

The ability to execute a task is a very important leadership trait. A leader must be able to develop strategies for the implementation of a project, campaign, or movement. A leader must be able to weigh the risk while being clear on the objective of the task at hand. A leader must be circumspect enough to deliver on a project on time, on budget, and on quality. A leader must be able to replicate program efforts consistently, transparently, selflessly, and without procrastination. The people are always watching and so, as leaders, we must be an example of the change we want to see in our world.

One of the other movements I am involved in is called ARTvocacy. It does not require that the youth go on the streets to march. Rather, it is a movement that uses all forms of the creative arts as a tool to advocate for social justice. The ART-vocacy movement was launched in the city of Abuja in 2021. This movement was designed by Street Project Foundation in collaboration with Enugu Youth Entrepreneurship Network (EYEN) with the support of VOICE, a funding program, in response to the insecurity that people who exercise their rights marching on the streets experience. As such, what we do is to activate youth in different cities of the country by strengthening their capacity in community organizing, movement building, and content development. After the activation, the youth groups are able to scale up the movement in their communities so that in time, we have a critical mass of young creatives using their art forms to challenge the government, community leaders, and citizens of the country through socially conscious content that can influence their decisions.

During my convening with the youth, I always spend time with those who struggle with procrastination and those who start a project and don't finish it. Our youth convenings serve as Zones of Proximal Development (ZPDs) to support and strengthen the capacity of the youth to undertake revolutionary projects like the ARTvocacy movement, from start to finish. One way we condition our youth to change their mindset about work is through the "pressure cooker projects."

I'll often tell them to come up with a group name and chants and I give a bunch of strangers meeting themselves for the very first time the opportunity to agree on a name and chant. The duration is often a five-minute time frame. Their immediate response is, "It's impossible," however when they start to embark on the task, they find a way because of the pressure of time.

Another task that I engage the youth in is what I call "creating your identity." When groups are formed and they have their names and chants, I push them further to come up with a vision statement starting the sentence with "I see a world where…" They then go a step further to draw, paint, design, or create a symbol that represents their ideology and the vision they have set for themselves. This is done under the pressure of a ten-minute time limit. The task is hardly ever completed within the time frame, as such the essence of this task is to get them started on a much more long-term group project.

These are samples of bite-sized tasks that I get them to do to stretch their mental muscles for "doing." However, when the task is completed, we then reflect on the process of getting that pressure cooker project done, such as the upsides and downsides. The generic feedback I get after these sessions are statements like, "I thought it was impossible and so surprised we were able to do it. I love my team." During the process of reflection, we also see teams struggling with their group dynamics and it becomes a learning opportunity for everyone else to understand the cracks in their relationship building and elements in highly functioning groups that could be replicated in their groups to enable them to get their projects done.

Youths who undergo our programs are always saddled with a practical project that must be completed before their graduation. This task is a part of our curriculum because it is a deliberate attempt to stop the pattern of procrastination. They are expected to memorize this quote:

> "Excuses are the tools of the incompetent, a monument of nothingness; those who use them are not wise."
>
> —(ADEFARASIN, 2022)

Whenever a project which was started by a youth group is successfully completed, it's a sign for me and my team that they are set to perform as revolutionaries. It could be taking up a political position in school or becoming a member of an advisory board like some of our youth have attained already. It is a sign that they will become culture creators and social change agents that will co-create a world of inclusivity, pluralism, and social cohesion.

Community organizing requires resilience and passion. It is an opportunity for citizens to understand their collective power in causing a shift that will impact a nation positively. #BlackLivesMatter movement is top of mind right now and the impact is so visible in the current trend of things. It is a movement that has inspired other movements like the #EndSARS movement in Nigeria, which is a fight to end police brutality by the Special Anti-Robbery Squad set up across states in Nigeria.

According to a March 15, 2022, publication by Adaugo Pamela Nwakanma, this is reiterated:

As Nigerian youth took to the streets to demand justice, police reform, and government accountability, the Black Lives Matter movement continued to gain momentum and shape public discourse in ways that propelled issues of racial inequality and state violence to the center of American politics following the publicized police murders of Breonna Taylor, George Floyd, Ahmaud Arbery, and numerous others. Originating in response to the acquittal of George Zimmerman in the murder of Trayvon Martin in 2013, Black Lives Matter is a decentralized socio-political movement and global network that organizes and builds local power to "intervene in violence inflicted on Black communities by the state and vigilantes" (Black Lives Matter 2021). Through its multilayered grassroots approach, the Black Lives Matter movement has successfully shifted police brutality from the margins of American politics to a much more prominent position (Freelon et al. 2018). And this effect is seen beyond the United States in various parts of the world.

I am quick to learn, however, that organizing anything takes time. It's an intentional activity. Structures are required, and the coming together of people with a common purpose is essential to its existence and sustenance. With consistency, you are bound to reach your tipping point.

Community organizing is not for the lily-livered. Oftentimes it may seem like a daunting task but as long as you don't lose sight of your focus and believe in the cause you are fighting for or against, you must keep pressing on. When organizing a community for a cause, you may not see the result in your lifetime. It happens for some people but not all. Moses in the Bible had a life purpose to set his people free and lead them to the Promised Land. He started the process and strategically migrated his people out of Egypt, however, when it was time, he saw the Promised Land but did not get to enter it. It was Joshua who ended up fulfilling that mission.

Your fight for a policy change may not come in the first five years of the movement but, no matter how slow it seems, you are moving the needle on the cause you care about when you organize. Ask Stacey Abrams, an American voting rights activist, and Tarana Burke, the American activist who started the Me Too movement.

NOT TOO YOUNG TO BE COMMUNITY ORGANIZERS

To the passionate and vibrant youth of Nigeria who organized communities online and on the streets to protest, it may seem like it wasn't a successful #EndSARS movement. For me, however, it was a sign of the development of Gen Z and Millennials toward active citizenship and political participation. You moved the needle.

Organizing the community into movements for social change may not seem like it has an immediate impact, but changes can happen over time. Case in point, the "Not Too Young to Run" bill passed in July 2017.

"Not Too Young to Run," arguably Nigeria's largest youth-led movement, is an open campaign that seeks to promote the rights of young people running for public office. The campaign, which started in 2016, sought to reduce legal age of candidacy for key political positions to encourage more young people to seek office (Salaudeen, 2018).

The coalitions leading the youth-based campaign took their advocacy to social media and got millions of Nigerians to back the movement using the #NotTooYoungToRun hashtag. Following a lot of pressure and hard work, the bill was eventually passed. The assented bill brought down the age qualification for president from forty to thirty, house of representatives membership from thirty to twenty-five, and state house of assembly membership from thirty to twenty-five (Egbas, 2018).

On March 14, 2018, young people under the aegis of Youth Initiative for Advocacy, Growth, and Advancement, or YIAGA, were led to the Aso Rock gates by Samson Itodo. They had one mission in mind—pile the pressure on Buhari to sign the piece of legislation. The "Not Too Young to Run" movement issued President Buhari an eight-day ultimatum to assent to the bill. In the words of the movement: "The movement requested the President bequeath to Nigerian youth a memorable democracy gift by assenting to the 'Not Too Young to Run' bill" (Adaoyichie, 2018).

President Muhammadu Buhari, at the Presidential Villa on May 31st, 2018, made history. He assented to the "Not Too Young to Run" bill (Channels Television, 2018).

Community organizing is a process that requires resilience, tact, networking, and skill. It isn't an easy process, but it is worth it. The results are not immediate, but the wins happen in small dozes and what is important is to celebrate every milestone on the path to progress and social change—#WeMove.

CHANGE MAKER
- Tell your youth group to identify a problem in their community.
- Tell them to proffer a solution.
- Tell them to create a prototype of the solution using materials in their immediate environment to design.
- Give them a time frame of thirty minutes. The goal isn't for them to finish the task but to experience the process of getting the job done.
- When the time is up, go around from group to group to hear about their process.

CHAPTER SEVEN

QUEEN BEE

———

Voices of people I love in my head
Dissenting voices of naysayers in my head
Palpitations of my heartbeat vibrating in my head
the symphony of anxiety triggers my fingers to quiver
and palms to sweat,
uncertain what this orchestra of
mixed instruments will bring
Should I be one with the sound
Or should I be invisible?

"I too know."

This is a colloquial and derogatory way of saying one is highly opinionated or inquisitive.

Growing up in Nigeria, I often wondered why as kids we were shut down when we asked so many questions. When I asked why, I heard, "this is how we know it to be," "it's our culture," "it's our doctrine," and "it's the system; we cannot change it." These were phrases spoken by family members, relatives, religious leaders, and community leaders mostly during my teens to early twenties.

Martin Luther King dared to question racism and prejudice in the United States of America. Mandela dared to question Apartheid in South Africa. Fela dared to question the corrupt leadership in Nigeria and the continent of Africa. Malala Yousafzai dared to question a society averse to educating women. Harriet Tubman dared to question slavery. Dietrich Bonhoeffer dared to question Nazi Germany. Chimamanda Ngozi Adichie dared to question womens' role in the world. Jesus Christ dared to question religious sects that were quick to judge. Coco Chanel dared to question the corseted silhouette fashion of her time. Steve Jobs dared to question personal computers. Larry Page and Sergey Brin dared to question the conventional search engines of their time.

Anyone known to bring about social change or reform dared to question the status quo. I dare say that the world is shaped by those who are fearless enough to ask the right questions. This is why, now more than ever before, we must be intentional about raising youth leaders through new and innovative strategies like engaging with questions and dialogue, especially in the global south.

Here's to the crazy ones. The misfits. The rebels. The troublemakers. The round pegs in the square holes. The ones who see things differently. They're not fond of rules. And they have no respect for the status quo. You can quote them, disagree with them, glorify, or vilify them. About the only thing you can't do is ignore them. Because they change things. They push the human race forward. And while some may see them as the crazy ones, we see genius. Because the people who are crazy enough to think they can change the world, are the ones who do.
(SILTANEN, 2022)

This poem was made popular through the advertising of the Apple brand. It is an ode to the crazy ones, the troublemakers, the pacesetters. In this chapter, we will be taking a deep dive into understanding the process and result of youth development in the global south.

When I started Street Project Foundation with the premise of using the creative arts for the social transformation of youth, it seemed far-fetched at the time, especially given that I was very young and idealistic. Many thought it was a passing phase, but it was more than that; it was a conviction even when there were many unknown variables at play. To get people to buy into the vision of youth development using the creative arts as a tool required that I build influence, that I become a queen bee.

THE RESCUE

A landlord, after two years of allowing bees to infest his backyard, felt the need to call an exterminator to clear them out. His new tenants wouldn't have it and felt the need to call a bee expert to save the bees instead. I found the process of migrating the bee colony to a new environment intriguing. At first the bee expert was moving whatever she could remove from the old hive to the new hive. After moving the comb, she started to scoop the gentle bees into the new hive. The moment she moved them, they marched right in. Then more bees started to move into the new hive. She waited patiently for about fifteen minutes and then, she found the queen.

She picked up the queen bee with a clip and moved her to the new hive. Some bees then started sending signals to help the other bees find their way to the new hive where the queen bee was relocated. She left the hive in the shed overnight and when she returned the entire colony had migrated into the new hive (Texas Beeworks, 2021). Without the queen bee, the migration would have taken so much more time or might not have been successful at all.

The queen bee was very crucial to the change that the new tenants and bee experts wanted to achieve. For us to rescue people from the status quo we need influencers that have the capacity to move people emotionally, inspire them intellectually, and be charismatic enough for them to be influenced by their life examples. To become "Queen Bee," you must be a leader that does not feel threatened by questions but views them as a development tool for growth for the youth and for yourself. A leader who is open to seeing things from different perspectives and fosters an environment where no one's opinion is belittled, castigated, or maligned.

This kind of leadership is what Lev Vygotsky's calls the Zone of Proximal Development, or the ZPD. I was introduced to Vygotsky by Lois Holzman, the co-founder of East Side Institute New York, during my time as a student of the International Class. The Zone of Proximal Development is referred to as the space between what a learner can do without assistance and what a learner can do with adult guidance or in collaboration with more capable peers. ZPD is best experienced in a group therapy session, where the leader of the session is more a navigator of the conversation as opposed to the dominant voice in the conversation. The leader navigates the group by probing. The leader asks thought-provoking questions that make the group look at concepts, ideologies, and their opinions about an area of interest differently.

I like to think of myself as the Queen Bee of the youth spaces I curate. I am more of a listener and observer, looking for the perfect opportunity to create Zones of Proximal Development and collective teachable moments. My queenly expression happens often during Reflection Sessions: our innovative circle of trust where culture creators perform who they are, who they are not, and who they are becoming through immersive storytelling using various art forms.

As the Queen Bee, I am not prescriptive in my approach to leadership, rather I aid the creation of a probing environment that inspires the youth to think. According to an August 2021 article by Melissa Eisler, she states, "In order to encourage your team to get into a mode of thinking more innovatively, you have to ensure you set the right context and environment so it is highly conducive for creative thinking."

There are two things I am most concerned about during my sessions with the youth. The first is the environment where the sessions take place and the second is the context in which the youth have been assembled.

SETTING THE ENVIRONMENT

The environment where our youth programs are conducted is either in a physical space or a virtual space.

For a physical space, you should ensure that the location chosen is relatively a safe space. In Nigeria, most facilities have guards at the gates and some facilities have CCTV cameras that can track the ins and outs of individuals within their premises. It should also be spacious enough in width and height to embark on a variety of creative activities. I often avoid spaces with a lot of pillars due to dance sessions and theatre performances. We also ensure that the facility is suitable for the variety of creative activities lined up for the duration of our youth convening and boot camps, which involves dance, drama, visual arts, music, artistic upcycling, and the likes. We look out for open spaces, high enough for a summersault routine and spacious enough for uninhibited group activities.

For a remote meeting, however, ensure you have collected the names and emails of all registered participants and facilitators or curators before the meetings. With this information, the technology support team can track participants joining the virtual forum. Ensure you have sufficient data and bandwidth to share videos and music. This is a youth space, and even when you run programs online, they must be engaging, full of good vibes, and have no dull moments. Encourage participants to activate their video cameras from time to time within the session to trigger some level of human connection.

For physical spaces, the first thing we look out for structurally is accessibility for persons with disabilities. Are there ramps or elevators? Are the toilets wide enough and spacious enough for wheelchair users? It's quite tough to find facilities that meet accessibility standards in some parts of the global south where disability rights acts are still in their infancy with little or no implementation of the bills passed. In this case, we find a middle ground. There have been instances where disability rights activists in Nigeria issued a query to a hotel facility for its lack of accessibility and in less than a week, a ramp was constructed at the entrance of that facility. This does not happen all the time and so we decide on what's most important for the gathering based on the collective of the youth and persons with disability selected for the program. It is also advantageous to rent a facility not far from a hospital or medical center for emergencies.

For virtual meetings, we provide reasonable accommodations such as sign language interpreters as well as close captions for the hearing impaired. For the visually impaired, we ensure that the documents shared are compatible with accessibility apps on mobile devices, laptops, and desktops. We also ensure facilitators do well to explain their slides and talk about the visual representations that the visually impaired are unable to see. This enables them to enjoy the experience as well as everybody else.

You may ask what a space has got to do with being a Queen Bee. In the part of the world where I come from, it's critical. Our young people are aspirational, and you do not want them in an environment that reminds them of where they come from, which is one of deprivation. Rather, you want them in an environment that inspires them to be more than what they are, a space that makes them dream and strive for greatness. Creating a comfortable environment makes the conversations and co-creation activities even more enjoyable.

Youth need safe public spaces where they can come together, engage in activities related to their diverse needs and interests, participate in decision making processes and freely express themselves. Safe public spaces such as civic spaces enable youth to engage in governance issues; public spaces afford youth the opportunity to participate in sports and other leisure activities in the community; digital spaces help youth interact virtually across borders with everyone; and well-planned physical spaces can help accommodate the needs of diverse youth especially those vulnerable to marginalization or violence (Youth Power 2, 2022).

In an article published in July 2020 by Ikenna Chidiebere Anyadike, she states,

The importance of safe spaces for young people in the 21st century cannot be over-emphasized, due in part to the results that have been recorded from experiments carried out by examining the outcome(s) of young people who experienced safe spaces

against those who did not. A Safe Space functions as a break between school and home, and to be honest, it is a break from school and home. They are safe and healthy and offer secure environments where young people get to meet their peers from other communities and schools. They get to pan out and relax, watch television, play board games, undertake and explore life lessons that don't necessarily get covered in school. Simply put, safe spaces are crucial because they are friendly.

When the location has been set and your program is ready to commence, ensure that you make the first day the most memorable. Teens and young adults tune out easily these days. Born into a digital world, they are used to what we call the "microwave lifestyle": fast and furious. A good number of them come into the space with a preconceived mindset of "If this isn't exciting, I'll end it immediately as I have no time to waste," especially if the gathering is free of charge and they have nothing to lose.

The first day sets the tone for the duration of the program. As such, ensure the ambiance of the venue is stimulating. The use of visual elements like banners and posters with clear messages about the program are available. Kit them up if you can with branded T-shirts and name tags. Branded notebooks and pens help to elevate their expectations. The air conditioning should be just right and there should be popping colors to stimulate their senses and inspire them to create. Above all, make sure you have a Queen Bee.

In Nigeria, despite over 70 percent of its population being thirty years old and under, the infrastructure for credible and viable youth resource centers is almost nonexistent. We are missing hubs for creative arts programming, sports centers, and public libraries (Fayehun and Isiugo-Abanihe, 2022).

As a part of our development strategy at Street Project Foundation, before commencing any youth program, it is important to secure a safe environment. As of June 20, 2022, a permanent structure of our own does not exist, so we scout for the right facility in any location we decide to implement a project.

SETTING THE CONTEXT

The Queen Bee in the space sets the context in which the teens and young adults operate. This is where the creative arts play a crucial role. With strategic play exercises, we are able to co-create the conversations that take place in the space. Activities that make them listen to one another, draw, paint, sing, dance, and speak publicly are crucial for engagement.

The teenage years are the time when there's an urgency to be free and independent. The desire to live life the way we want to. These are years when hormones run wild and fast when we struggle with our emotions and lack the mastery of not allowing our feelings to cloud our sense of judgment. Healthy cultivation of youth development in communities is a necessity, not a resource to be created as a reactive measure to the sudden increase in teenage pregnancies, juvenile crimes, or a rise in suicide.

Just like the Queen Bee, for any kind of meaningful change to happen, we need leaders that we can depend on, leaders that followers instinctively gravitate toward. Now more than ever before, I understand why a beehive appears wherever Beyoncé performs. It is her creative leadership through consistency, discipline, and innovation that makes her fans gravitate toward her because she always reinvents herself and her performance, keeping it fresh for her fans. In like manner, years after his death, there remains a growing hive for Fela Kuti's Afrobeat style and, beyond his unique sound, the catalyst for his following is the fact that he stood for a cause that was larger than himself. He questioned the government through his music in ways that not many artists had the audacity to do at the time.

As a youth development practitioner, you must be passionate about setting an agenda where the process of becoming is as important as the result of becoming. In the global south where questioning your elders is seen as disrespectful, we must dare to change that status quo by encouraging the youth in our communities to ask questions and create an environment that serves as a youth hive. We set the context by creating intentional activities that make our youth conversationalists and not just receptors of instructions. By making our youth conversationalists, we disrupt the trend of them becoming consumerists and adopters of culture. Rather, they become curious, conscious, and confident enough to become co-creators of a culture of social change in our society.

PLAYING WITH COMMONALITIES

In this game, our commonality is the gravitational force that pulls people to one another just like the Queen Bee is influential in changing locations and ideas. I also love playing this game when I want to break a large grouping of the youth into subgroups of four or five. It makes them move from one end of the hall to another to keep their energy up.

1. Divide the room into two halves. Label one X and the other O.
2. Make the youths pick a side of the room based on things they like or dislike. For example: "Early birds move to X. Night owls move to O." You can also make the kids

perform certain actions: "If you love to run every morning, frog jump to X. If you love fashion, catwalk to O."

In split seconds, people can see what they have in common with others in their group. This exercise is also fun to do with a collection of youth meeting each other for the very first time. You can also divide the room into four parts or more if you have a bigger group and create more variables, such as those who are indifferent about what they like or those who don't like any of the options provided.

CHAPTER EIGHT

A SPROUT IS COMING

———

Let's talk about dreams.

The process takes time, but the result is magical.

Dreams are like seeds: the full potential of what they can become will only materialize when it is planted, and it is fully grown.

The process of planting isn't an easy one. Even preparing the ground in which the seed will be planted is a tedious exercise. The truth is some grounds may not be good enough for your seed to grow. Often times it's a lonely process navigating new grounds. My pastor, Paul Adefarasin, will often say, "Apple trees cannot grow in warm climates like the city of Lagos. Apple trees can only grow under the conditions they were designed to grow: cold climates." The process of growing an organization like the Street Project Foundation meant I needed to be fearless enough to make mistakes. Daring enough to fail and get back up again and again. Humble enough to learn from my mistakes and rebuild again. Essential for building an initiative and organization designed to last is to never stop doing things again;

you might change your strategy and methods but what is important is consistency.

The more messy the grounds are, the more fertile it becomes for the seed to thrive. Experts say one of the signs of fertile soil is the presence of plenty of underground animals and plant activity. Need I say more about what the seed goes through underground? However, what I have come to learn is that the process one goes through in the days when you are not seen, when you are invisible, is the period when your capacity is stretched and strengthened at the same time. Making you prepared for that day when your dreams are no longer hidden.

The process of developing, creating, and bringing ideas to life takes dedication and time.

According to an article published in October 2019 by Carolyn Gregoire, a writer and creative consultant, there are four stages to the creative process: Preparation, Incubation, Illumination, and Verification. She says:

Any creative process is a dance between the inner and the outer; the unconscious and conscious mind; dreaming and doing; madness and method; solitary reflection and active collaboration [...]. Through a dynamic dance of inspiration and generation, brilliant work comes to life.

Don't give up because of the mess you've found yourself planting your dream in the hearts and minds of people who may not just get it, yet. I tried to give up a couple of times, especially because of the limited financial resources required to give life to my dream. What has been my driving force is my holistic connection to the vision of the organization and its alignment with my life's purpose.

Disconnecting from the dream of the Street Project Foundation in the initial stages was like cutting off my air supply. Secondly, a support system of "yaysayers" as opposed to naysayers and having a solid fan base of family and friends aids one's ability to stick to the cause. Sometimes people won't believe in your vision, but they might believe in your capabilities to make things happen. Having such people can be a militating factor against quitting the implementation of your dreams and a catalyst to prove to them that your dreams are valid.

VISUALIZING YOUR DREAMS

"When you visualize, then you materialize."

—DENIS WAITLEY

When I thought of fully committing to the development of the idea called Street Project Foundation, I was on my third job as a manager in an advertising firm. After work hours, I made time to write down the vision of the Street Project Foundation and map out how I wanted it to be run. To stimulate my passion even further, I briefed my colleague at the time, Chuka Obi, about the vision of the organization and what I wanted the brand identity of the organization to look like. I practically wanted a graffiti representation to show the irreverent DNA of the organization. Chuka, being the awesome creative artist that he was, sketched the idea of what would become the identity of Street Project Foundation today. It was a pencil sketch but it was enough to excite me, enough to keep me awake at night, enough to keep me thinking about the many things I wanted to achieve and how.

Visualizing your dream is a way by which you can fertilize your seed. My mind is stimulated quickly by designs, pictures, paintings, and symbols, so when I am nursing an idea, I like to have them represented in such formats before I start to write about them.

Research shows that the average reaction time to a visual stimulus is 0.25 seconds (Backyard Brains, 2022).

What is important is to look for a stimulus that works for you to keep you focused on your dream.

After I had looked at the sketch long enough, I was inspired to write. I visualized the future in a PowerPoint presentation where I reflected on the vision and mission of the organization, the members of the team, and their roles and responsibilities were spelled out. Having things written down gave me a blueprint of how to share my ideas with people in my network. Facebook at the time had only been around for four years before I joined, and it became my first office. There, I shared the dream of the Street Project Foundation with as many people in my network. Yes, a network is a very important resource for builders, seed planters, visionaries, and creators. I often come across people who say "I'm not a people's person" or "I just like to be in my own corner." My question then would be, so whom are you creating for? Whom are you dreaming for? Whom are you building for?

I wasn't always Queen Bee, as I expressed in Chapter Seven. I had to learn how to become a woman who people gravitate to. The advantages of being bold and confident far outweighed being timid and shy. I decided to put myself out there because that was the only way I would learn how to build a formidable and resourceful network of people. It is within your network that you'll find helpers for your vision.

CULTIVATING RELATIONSHIPS

> "Everything you want in life
> is a relationship away."

—IDOWU KOYENIKAN

I couldn't agree more with the above quote. Networking is a crucial tool for the materialization of your dreams. Often, I'll engage our youth community with what I call "the pretend game." The idea of the game is to get people to playfully learn about each other by pretending to be like the person who they just met. They get to meet one person and listen to each other keenly. For their next introduction, however, they pretend to be the person they just met; they take on their persona and introduce themselves as that other person. Most often it breaks the ice because of how silly it makes them feel and it breaks down their walls so that they are able to connect with more people.

In the same way, we take team building seriously during our creative youth boot camps because we view these exercises as critical moves for the youth to build a connected community. This is so that before they leave the camp, they become a part of a formidable network of like-minded youth. As a result of this network, they get to access information easily, canvass for votes for a competition they are a part of, and collaboration for artistic endeavors like filmmaking, spoken word and musical fusions, stage plays, and more. They form what could be called a community of practice.

While on Facebook, I was able to build my network and engage my network of family, friends, and acquaintances. My first project was created with two colleagues working in the same advertising firm. We agreed to christen our first initiative A Smile for December. We visited a hospice. Fundraising was done both online and offline. I remember investing half of my salary to the cause. I produced about one hundred branded T-shirts and sold out most of the T-shirts to colleagues in my office, friends, and family who came across my fundraising campaign on Facebook. This was how I was able to start replicating what I envisioned in my mind.

When you ask the youth what's stopping them from implementing their dreams, oftentimes you'll get a reply, "money." As much as money is a fuel to implement your dreams, the greatest resource is yourself. Note I didn't have the funds to execute my first project. I had to ask myself what I had. At the time, what I had was a very youth-centric logo and a Facebook platform with a couple of followers who were true fans of my work. So, with a few samples of T-shirts produced and advertised on my page and in my work community, I was able to raise the funds I needed for the visit to the hospice.

For the next project, I leveraged relationships I had formed with clients in the food and beverage industry. This time, I didn't have to sell T-shirts; all I did was write and send letters. I then followed up with my contacts in the organizations and donations of company products and branded items were given. This fundraising pattern for in-kind donations now became the model we replicated for the implementation of A Smile for December.

CONSISTENCY

For your dream to be seen, you must be consistent. You should be known for that idea above everything else. I nursed my dream so much that when friends and colleagues meet me at a function, the first question they'd ask was, "How is the Street Project?" At some point, I'd have to remind them that I was still a marketing communications practitioner.

Your dream sprout is like the tip of an iceberg: before it can be seen, all the hard work of building is done in places that people cannot see. They all form the hard crust under the sea. This is what holds the core of your dream together so that no matter how big your dream becomes, you remain grounded.

Don't get it twisted: Implementing a project when you have limited resources is not easy. It is key to have people in your corner who don't necessarily have to provide the funds but can key into the idea well enough to share their skills, knowledge, and network. Everything isn't money, but money is important in the success of growing a youth movement. As such, it is very crucial to have someone in your team who thinks about grants, financial growth, and sustainability and has the requisite skill to source funds. In my case, I got married to a resource mobilizer and this life partnership with my husband, Ezenwa Okoro, was a turning point for the organization. Also, in my corner was someone who understands finance, the movement of money, expenditure, liabilities, and assets: a requisite skill for a not-for-profit due to the essential need for accountability. Fortunately, Eduvie, my bestie for over two decades with a banking and finance background, came to the rescue. With these two key partnerships in place, Street Project Foundation was set to grow in leaps and bounds. The lesson here is if you don't have money, surround yourself with human assets.

"Courage is the most important of all the virtues because without courage, you can't practice any other virtue consistently."

—MAYA ANGELOU

In the process of making your dreams come true, you must be resilient and avoid procrastinating the implementation of your ideas so you can build a track record that makes you and your work visible. However, there is another perspective to the conversation about making your dreams visible: gender. Gender can be a limiting factor, but there are people who against all odds have risen above the stereotypes of gender and built up their courage to ensure that their dreams materialize regardless.

CONVERTING SHIT TO FUEL

Leila Hoteit, the global leader of Boston Consulting Groups' education, employment, and welfare sector once told a story about how she and her daughter were in Dubai and having passed by the picture of the three leaders of Dubai, her daughter asked, "We never see powerful women on the walls here in Dubai or in Lebanon [where her grandparent come from]. Are women not important?" She found this one of the hardest questions she had ever had to answer as a parent and professional with over sixteen years of experience under her belt. Her father, who was a pilot and director of operations of a Lebanese airline, ensured her sister and herself pursued an education despite the fact her culture emphasized that it was sons and not daughters who should be educationally motivated (Hoteit, 2022).

She was one of the few girls at age eighteen who traveled abroad to study mechanical engineering, a male-dominated field, and she never found role models that looked like her. She stated that "Arab women have had to become their own role models." Naturally, the word you think about when you read this may be "resilience." Her definition of resilience, however, is the ability to "convert her shit into fuel."

I really find that definition quite boisterous.

She was working with a man called John and worked hard to show him that she was worthy of being made a partner at the firm. Besides her consultancy work, she was working passionately toward women's economic empowerment.

One day she got to present her research to a room full of MBA students. John was there listening for the first time to the details of her findings. Whilst he listened, he slid under his chair in apparent shame.

After she was applauded for her presentation and they got into the car, he raised his voice and stated that what she did was unacceptable, stating that she was a consultant and not an activist. He added that when women have children, their place is in the home. Time stood still and she said to herself, "You can forget about the partnership, Leila; it's never going to happen."

However, after she reflected, she came up with the following deductions. These were his issues, his complexes, and she would never make his issues her issues. She needed a new sponsor, and she needed one fast. She had to show John what women with children can do.

This story moves me so much when I reflect on it. I believe that this is an approach that anyone who has been discriminated against due to gender, class, and more should explore. The battlefield of the mind is where these wars take place. It's left for us to find our strength to deal with naysayers who don't believe in our dreams. You need to show them what a person with a dream can achieve.

I didn't always have people in my corner. Sometimes people would act like they were but when the time came to act, they were nowhere to be found. In fact, much later I found out that some people I looked up to thought I would crash and burn because of how idealistic my dream sounded and because of my unfathomable optimism. I'm glad I turned the shit of unbelief to fuel; I can share with concrete evidence that it pays off. Today, Street Project Foundation is an award-winning organization, recognized by the United Nations Alliance of Civilization (UNAOC) and the BMW Group. A dream that started with seed has grown and begun to blossom. When people see the magic of the result, they often forget that there was a process that required patience, doggedness, and sheer power of will.

In summary, don't give up on your dreams because of the mess around. Find ways to visualize your dreams so that it serves as a stimulus for you to keep going.

Search for your allies, yaysayers, and naysayers, and use their words as fuel for your journey in good times or bad times.

UPCYCLING

This activity is inspired by the work of a friend and sister, Ife Abhulimen, who also is a member of the faculty of the Street Project Foundation's Creative Youth Boot Camp. She inspires our young people to transform trash into treasure and waste into wealth.

1. Tell your community of supporters to donate their recyclable waste to your boot camps. It could be plastic, fabric, or furniture.
2. Pour out a collection of recyclable waste products in the middle of the room and supply your young people with art supplies.
3. Count to ten.
4. After ten, the youth have ten seconds to run to the middle of the circle to grab the waste they intend to upcycle.
5. Give them a thirty-minute time limit to create something of value.
6. Give them two minutes each to present their creation explaining what problem they intended to solve, their process of creation, and the name of their creation.

Remember, like with other exercises, the focus should be on the process, not just the result. Ensure everyone is celebrated for their efforts.

CHAPTER NINE

MENTAL HEALTH

The world is mad.

If you are up to date with news across the world, you'll come to this very same conclusion. As of June 21, 2022, this was breaking news across the world: 320 victims are dead in an Ethiopian gun attack. Belgium returns Patrice Lumumba's tooth to the family sixty-one years after his murder. Sudanese museums seek the return of artifacts taken by British colonizers. Two Canadians were found dead in Playa del Carmen Mexican beach resort. Russia attacks Ukraine. Floods in Assam submerge entire villages. Man held in police custody after woman and daughter fatally stabbed in London (The Guardian, 2022).

Should we discuss the constant news of shootings in the US or Boko Haram insurgencies in Nigeria? Every day, we are encumbered with news that reflects the state of the world today. As such, I often wonder about our averseness to the state of mind of people whose realities of the world are termed delusional.

In the world today, racism is a topical issue born out of biases that make one human being feel they are superior to another human being because of the color of their skin. This in and of itself is a mental health issue. This fact is corroborated by mental health and wellness experts (Mental Health America, 2022).

Racism is a mental health issue because racism causes trauma. And trauma paints a direct line to mental illnesses, which need to be taken seriously (Mental Health America, 2022).

In like manner, people have biases against persons who exhibit mental health challenges. In Nigeria, mental health issues are still viewed largely as spiritual issues as opposed to both spiritual and biological. As such, you may come across religious sects that whip the said "demons" out of a person who may be schizophrenic, bipolar, autistic, dyslexic, or suffering from panic attacks.

Nigeria's 1958 Lunacy Act allows the detaining of people with mental health conditions in mental health institutions, even without providing medical or therapeutic treatment (NSW Legislation, 2022). People spend years in institutions—sometimes decades—because Nigeria lacks adequate services to support them in the community. In all but one of the institutions Human Rights Watch visited, people were not allowed to leave or to challenge their detention.

Human Rights Watch found that people with actual or perceived mental health conditions, including children, are placed in facilities without their consent, usually by relatives. In some cases, police arrest people with actual or perceived mental health conditions and send them to government-run rehabilitation centers. Once there, many are shackled with iron chains to heavy objects or to other detainees, in some cases for months or years. They cannot leave, are often confined in overcrowded, unhygienic conditions, and are sometimes forced to sleep, eat, and defecate within the same confined place. Many are physically and emotionally abused as well (Human Rights Watch, 2020).

Mental illness is considered shameful in this part of the world because of the stigma. As such, a culture of silence is the order of the day in the treatment of mental health challenges. The thought of managing the stigma and shame and everything associated with mental health challenges makes it even more difficult to solve the problem. The only people in the space of a person with mental health in this context are traditional and modern "spiritual leaders." A mix of concoctions, rituals, and prayers to exorcise the supposed demons is the prescription to stop the delusion.

The issue of mental health is very close to home. I had a loved one who screamed at things that we couldn't see with our physical eyes. Episodes would last for a period and then normalcy returned again. This would go on for years and the only remedy at the time were prayers, shaving of the hair, and palm fronds for whipping the delusion out.

According to a CNN report published on October 10, 2020, by Aisha Salaudeen:

One of the reasons people visit religious and traditional healing centers for mental illness is a lack of understanding of mental health issues in the country, according to Dr. Orjinta. Dr. Orjinta, told CNN that in many cases, Nigerians seek mental health care from unorthodox places, especially religious centers before considering going to the hospital.

However, delaying mental care by not immediately going to hospital prolongs the time the patient stays without appropriate care and "may create the worst outcome for the patient as they have more symptoms," she said. "There is still a stigma around mental illness. People perceive it in a negative light and as a result, they don't want to address it if they have symptoms. They want to keep on hiding it," she explained. She also added there aren't enough mental health professionals in the country, making it difficult to access mental health care. For example, with a population of more than 200 million people, there are only 250 practicing psychiatrists in the country.

There is a disproportionate sharing of mental health professionals, we don't really have them in rural areas. And if someone lives in such areas without mental health care, of course, they will find alternatives for care like traditional healers or churches," Dr. Orjinta explained (Salaudeen, 2020).

With all said, how does the systemic infusion of creative arts support a country and continent where the treatment and awareness of mental health are limited?

POETIC HEALING

According to an interview I conducted with Steven T. Licardi, a spoken-word poet, social worker, and performance activist on my talk show, *Online With REO*, in May 2020. I shared my hope that one day, our society will be safe enough for sharing mental health stories in public forums. I hoped that one day the stigma attached to persons dealing with mental health issues or families who are saddled with the responsibility of managing the mental health of loved ones are not labeled as cursed, possessed, or untouchables. Steven said in our conversation, "People are afraid of what they do not know."

My response to that was if you do not know, seek knowledge.

Steven is a high-performing individual who has been on the autism spectrum all his life. Following talks with him, I deduced that one of the interesting things his parents did was not label his condition. Diagnosis happened only when he was all grown. However, he found succor in the process of writing poetry. I dare say that Steven's poems are one of the deepest and most thought-provoking I have come across. I figure that it is so because he writes from a very different perspective and spectrum than many of us.

His poems have become tools for "ARTivism" and "ARTvocacy" and in workshops, he shares some of his poetry writing techniques. One of such techniques is pulling themes from other people's poems and recreating your poetry piece using the themes. At one of such workshops I attended, one of the themes he prompted us to write about was "Come, who needs ties," and this is what I came up with in less than two minutes:

Love ties, family ties, friendship ties, kindred ties
Knowing that ties could make you choke
if they are not constantly adjusted, recreated or
redesigned to fit the here and now.
Come you who needs ties
and commune in unity.

It was quite an exhilarating experience being able to think through an idea and write down the first thought that came to mind. What I have come to realize is that it is important to find a creative outlet for our emotions. It is a fact that trauma affects the body as well as it affects the brain. As such, activities that encourage creative movements, dance, painting, and writing have proven to be therapeutic.

"Trauma is stored in the body, and the way that we've experienced it is not always easy to access verbally. We experience it in images, and art can let us express that experience," she explains. Leela R. Magavi, MD, a regional medical director for Mindpath Health, says, "Some adults who have endured sexual abuse and traumatic situations during their childhood have repressed their memories for so long that they do not recall what occurred. Art therapy allows them to piece together lost memories and heal, so they can achieve their goals and trust once again in relationships" (White, 2022).

It was with this background understanding and my less-than-one-year stint working with autistic children that I was able to empathize and relate with Steven's story about being diagnosed with autism and how poetry and spoken word became his therapy. Steven now travels the world, attending workshops where he teaches people the art of poetry.

ART THERAPY

At the start of one of our Creative Youth Boot Camps, one of the youth felt compelled to share her diagnosis of schizophrenia. It was a discretionary move to alert the coordinators of the camp just in case of an episode. In the beginning, opening up to the larger group during our reflection sessions at the very inception was not an option. However, as we continued to build our creative community of openness and nonjudgmental interactions, without being prompted, one day the youth shared her mental health struggles and how dance had become therapy.

In like manner, during the course of our boot camps, we have had young people share mental health conditions like dissociative identity disorder. Most often, the circle of trust created during our reflection sessions has become a dynamic space for sharing burning issues that they do not feel safe talking about with parents or close relatives around.

However, what I find fascinating is the use of art forms such as poetry, photography, music, dance, and creative writing that serve as outlets for sharing their abstract and deep thoughts. In this instance, one of our exercises, called Performance of a Lifetime, which I shared in Chapter Three, I find very therapeutic. With this exercise, the kids share their life stories through music, dance, visual arts, and various creative art expressions that don't necessarily require the direct narration of their experiences but rather an artistic one. Opening up the door to have conversations dramatically with everyone else in the group. In the process, they feel comfortable having an unprescriptive dialogue about the trauma in their life. The turning point for a lot of them is finding out that they are not alone. Many others have been through worse and are finding a way out of their trauma.

At other boot camps, the youth open up about dark places in their lives where they were sexually or domestically abused. All of these and more are some of the solemn moments where we reflect on our inclusive society. We find that in spaces like ours where we use the creative arts to facilitate performance, it becomes therapeutic, developmental, and liberating.

MENTAL HEALTH AWARENESS

In the year 2021, my husband and I got the opportunity to work with Paul R. Sachs, a member of Street Project Foundation's board of directors and a clinical psychologist based in Philadelphia, USA, on a project titled "*Alaafia,*" which is a Yoruba word meaning rest of mind or peace of mind. This project was funded by the United States Government through the Mandela Washington Fellowship Reciprocal Grant implemented by IREX. This fund gave my husband and I, being Mandela Washington Fellows: the opportunity to work with an American citizen on a project that will be mutually beneficial to our communities. The essence of the project was to create a conversation starter tool for youth groups in academic, religious, or informal settings. We had to create three vignettes that were reflective of the stories of three young people. As such, a focus group discussion had to be conducted and it was curated by Paul R. Sachs.

Three youths were selected from across cohorts of Street Project Foundation's programs and they consented to share the complexities of their lives as youths living in Nigeria. One is a single mother, another is a person with a disability, and the third is a student with an identity crisis. They shared the stigma associated with their various circumstances and how actions like journaling, performing a spoken-word piece, and simply being unashamed to talk about who they are has helped them cope with the vicissitudes of a very judgmental society.

Their stories were artistically performed by other youth within the Street Project Foundation community who observed the focus group sessions. The three vignettes are available on YouTube and a manual can also be downloaded to guide youth groups on ways to engage with the various themes that are addressed. This is expected to serve as an innovative awareness tool that makes people and communities hold conversations at various levels about mental health issues.

HOW ARE YOU DOING?

There's a place for medicine, therapy, and spiritual interventions in the holistic treatment of mental health. We cannot afford to have tunnel vision or be judgmental on this subject matter because of the complexity of the human mind and human existence. With all that's going on in our world today—wars, ethnic rivalry, and the pandemic—many have experienced some form of mental health challenges. In these times, just asking, "How are you?" is so important. We all need to do a self-check as youth development practitioners and youth leaders.

As developmentalists, we also go through our own mental health challenges and we have to coordinate groups of young people who are going through theirs as well. I find that being sincere about our emotions places us in an even better position to create with the cocktail of shared emotions, which I call "we-motions."

I find writing down my emotions very therapeutic. I find wailing, screaming, and crying out my emotions very therapeutic too because this way, I don't suppress anything. By creating with my emotions, I am able to reframe my story and begin to engage with my emotions from a different perspective.

As a youth organizer constantly engaging with youth across different backgrounds, mental health support has been in constant demand.

According to a report by World Health Organization (WHO), the dwindling economy and the harsh economic situation of the country has made more Nigerians contemplate suicide and even go as far as committing the act.

Psychologically, periods of economic depression leads to an increase in suicide rates. According to WHO, Nigeria has the highest rate of suicide and depression in Africa, the current rate of suicide in Nigeria is 9.50 percent out of 100, 000 people (Iwalaiye, 2021).

With the increasing reports of suicide cases and depression, the global south needs to take the issue of mental health seriously. One way to start addressing these issues is by intentionally investing in infrastructure where creative arts can be placed at the heart of communities for recreation, wellness, and development.

EMOTIONAL IDENTITY

I was inspired to create this exercise due to the constant request from my youth groups for emotional support. Being a communications expert with quite a fascination for semiotics, or the study of signs and symbols, I thought it would be exciting for me to create a visually stimulating exercise that makes people engage with their emotions in an artistic way.

1. Get your youth group to breathe in through their nose and breath out through their mouth.
2. Ensure they have plain paper and drawing materials. Let them know that this exercise isn't about showing off their artistic skills.
3. Tell them to draw a symbol of the negative emotions they are currently dealing with. When you give this instruction, ensure there's music playing in the background to lighten the mood. This exercise can run for five minutes.
4. When they are done with the above activity, ask them to draw another symbol to describe the positive emotions they are experiencing. Play mood music and let the activity run for another five minutes.
5. Now tell the group to now draw a symbol that represents the combination of both emotions. Play mood music and let the activity run for another five minutes.

6. After this is done, run a showcase of their emotional identity. Get each of them to share their emotional identity and the process of developing the symbol. Feel free to ask questions about what their fears were about the exercise and what the symbol represents. Also, find out what they intend to do with the emotions they described.

CHAPTER TEN

ESTRANGIER

Stranger things await.

My parents told me not to talk to strangers. What they did not tell me was talking to strangers is essential to human existence.

One day, I walked into the United States Consulate in Lagos, Nigeria, and I met a stranger. This was following an email and phone call I received a few weeks before about being a recipient of President Barack Obama's Mandela Washington Fellowship of the Young African Leaders Initiative. This fellowship was conceived to strengthen the capacity of young leaders in business, public service, and civic engagement in sub-Saharan Africa. This was done through a six-week program at a university in the United States of America and an eight-week internship with organizations in the United States of America and across other African countries. It was the year 2014 and I had spent six years running Street Project Foundation with very limited resources and had seen a significant impact across communities in Lagos State.

I was invited to a predeparture onboarding session organized by the US consulate in Lagos. There were about eighteen of us who received the fellowship in Southern Nigeria and over forty of us across Nigeria. We were the pioneer set and so it was a big deal for a lot of us. I wore a simple black dress that day. My hair, nails, and make-up were on fleek. When I looked at myself in the mirror before setting out, I knew I was good to go. I was feeling good about myself. When I walked into the lobby of the consulate, I was asked by a front desk officer to sit down, and then afterward, another officer came down to the lobby to lead me to join others who arrived before me.

There we were: strangers seated at a round table. Suddenly another stranger walked in and sat directly opposite me. He wasn't just any stranger. He reminded me of the male characters I read about in my Mills and Boons romance novels. He had dreamy eyes and a chiseled nose. He never took his eyes off me and started a conversation. Within a very short period, I could tell that he was resourceful, and he liked me. He looked so good, and I wanted him.

This stranger asked for my hand in marriage on day two of the predeparture onboarding session, in front of all other strangers I met the day before. Today, that stranger is my husband of seven years and counting. In these seven years, he has committed his time, talent, energy, and resources to the growth of the Street Project Foundation and with his support, numerous young lives have been transformed in Nigeria.

NETWORKING

One word that spans across both the marketing communications and development sectors is networking. My husband Ezenwa Okoro's networking abilities was one of the things that endeared me to him. I can tell you that I am on a life-long capacity-strengthening program with Ezenwa, who is an expert in networking. Networking is how we connect, become resourceful, and get things done more effectively. Most of my years have been invested in the process of converting strangers to acquaintances, sometimes friends who become a part of my network for a lifetime. I had to learn to be more open, to break the ice, and start conversations with people I ordinarily would prefer not to initiate a conversation with either because I felt intimidated by their position in an organization or biased about their outgoing lifestyle.

What life has taught me is that initiating conversations with people you do not know is a life skill every young person needs to learn. In the design of our youth development programs, I ensure that improvisational exercises are deployed to make our young people conversationalists. A January 2018 article by Monica Lake, PsyD, corroborates the need for the youth to be in groups to develop their social skills.

Social skills are an important aspect of life, so you may want to enroll your child in a social skills group. Groups are a great place to learn social skills because they typically provide direct instruction, modeling, role-playing, team building activities, and positive reinforcement.

A March 2018 blog post by the Learning Portal Team also corroborates this fact.

Social and emotional skills also factor into the learning objectives of the fourth Sustainable Development Goal for education. For example, the inclusion of "relevant and effective learning outcomes" in target 4.1 and "youth and adults who have relevant skills [...] for employment, decent jobs, and entrepreneurship," in target 4.4 alludes to not only cognitive skills but non-cognitive skills such as problem-solving, critical thinking, teamwork, and conflict resolution, among others.

REFLECTION SESSIONS

In the year 2019–2021, I was responsible for coordinating a project called Creative Youth Boot Camp: Art for Social Transformation, a six-week convening of the youth from underserved communities, gifted in different creative and performing art forms. This project was funded by VOICE Global. I worked with a total of one hundred youths in the space for a year and six months but divided into four batches of twenty-five youths for each cohort. As mentioned in Chapter Seven, creating a conducive environment for the youth to speak up freely and challenge the status quo without judgment was a big part of the design.

At the end of our six-hour intensive sessions each day, we would sit in a circle for what we refer to as "Reflection Sessions." This was a group therapy session that I learned by observing group therapy sessions during my social therapeutics study at East Side Institute, New York. Reflection Sessions is an avenue for the youth to play, perform, and share intimate stories with people they would ordinarily call strangers.

One exercise we get the youth to play with is called "the eye contact game." They stand opposite each other and look into each other's eyes for sixty seconds to one hundred and eighty seconds. Some of their immediate responses are laughter, abrupt avoidance of their partner's eyes, absolute discomfort, or a sheer desire to try the activity out even just to see who will blink first. After the exercise, I ask each of them to tell me what they could unravel about their partner's personality just by looking into their eyes. It is mind-blowing how much each person had to say about their partner. It's important to note that this exercise is usually one of the first bonding activities we deploy so that they transition from strangers to acquaintances quickly. It surprises them how much people can discern about us just by looking into our eyes. This breaks down their guard and helps them think about the concept of "strangers" differently.

The root word for strangers is a French word, *"estrangier,"* which means foreign or alien. I find "strangers" sounds judgmental when used to qualify a human being. What makes a human being foreign, alien, unknown, or an outsider? An object can be strange, and a location can be unfamiliar, but should humans be classified as aliens? If we all live in a shared universe, why do we call anyone alien?

According to the TED talk in September 2016 by Kio Stark, the author of *When Strangers Meet*,

The really sad thing is in many parts of the world we are raised to believe that strangers are dangerous by default, that we can't trust them and they might hurt us but most strangers aren't dangerous. We are uneasy around them because we have no context, we don't know what their intentions are, so instead of using our perception and making choices, we rely on this category of stranger.

She continues by saying that the two benefits of using our sense instead of our fears, is that it liberates us and brings about what she calls fleeting intimacy.

Researchers have found that people are more comfortable being honest and open about their inner selves with strangers than they do with their friends and families because they often feel more understood by strangers (BBC Radio 4, 2022). I find that this is the case when we run reflection sessions. The young participants of our boot camps are so open about issues related to abuse, poverty, inequalities experienced because of their gender or physical disability, and frictions with parents and family members.

This openness is possible for them because there are no consequences from close friends and relatives who have pre-conceived notions about them. Openness is easy during the session because when one person feels comfortable disclosing an issue, it gives others permission and freedom to share their own stories, which then brings about unexpected connections.

Another exercise that we explore is the exercise of listening. Our youth are put in pairs to have an improvisational conversation. They pick randomly from a bowl full of themes. They read it and they each take turns to talk on the theme but in a dialogue format and not a monologue. When one speaks, the other listens. In response, the other summarizes their partner's point and builds on it or counters their opinion constructively and respectfully. However, the essence of this exercise is to get the youth to have an unbiased conversation with only one rule: "Listen to understand, not to reply."

More than ever before, we need a generation of youth who listen. Stephen Covey states in his book *7 Habits of Highly Effective People*, "Most people do not listen with the intent to understand; they listen with the intent to reply," (Covey, 2004).

This is such an important exercise that every youth worker requires. Not just listening to what the youth say, but to their nonverbal communication as well. The way they move their hands, shiver, space out as they talk, tears and laughter are all part of the things we listen for. In like manner, we strengthen the youths' capacity to listen for understanding, empathy, and for action.

Listening is an intentional action. It's not an easy thing to do when there's so much noise in your head. However, it is an intentional action that can be learned. Listening affords us the opportunity to not close up on a single story about an issue but be open to more perspectives and form an informed opinion about a subject matter. Chimamanda Ngozi Adichie's speech on the dangers of a single story still rings true today (Adichie, 2009).

I believe strongly that the prevalence of violent extremism, white supremacy, xenophobia, and religious intolerance are all the effects of a closed society that refuses to open up to understand other people's views about a matter and settles to embrace one story and nothing else. When people appear different from us, it is developmental to listen to what they have to say, and if we clearly do not align with their school of thought, we can present a compelling argument when we clearly understand their point of view.

If there is anything the exercise on listening does, it helps us reflect on our interconnectedness as human beings and alienation of the concept of the enstrangier because our emotions and our spirits connect positively or negatively with people because of what we perceive about them. I find this exercise a step in the right direction to teach the youth tolerance and the capacity to respect each other's culture, beliefs, and opinions.

Kio Starks also mentioned something profound which aligns with my reflection about the words "alien" and "foreign." She says, "Using perception instead of categories is much easier said than done. Categories are the easy way out and it leads to a road of bias. It means we are thinking of people as individuals," (Stark, 2016).

To best explain this thought, I'll use this example. Imagine being in a room filled with able-bodied youth chatting away and being vivacious. Suddenly, a young lady wearing metal braces on her leg with crutches in hand walks in. The atmosphere is sure to change because, at that moment, she appears strange to everyone. The first thing that occurs is that they categorize or stereotype her by putting her in a box. Seeing her more than her disability requires an intentional activity and an awareness of the ability she possesses irrespective of her disability. When we allow our minds to think in diverse ways, it detracts us from the road of bias.

> ## "What unites us is much greater than what divides us."
>
> —POPE JOHN XXVIII

No one is exempt from the fact that as humans, we have our biases, and this is a wall that hinders growth and development. We must call ourselves to order when we realize the path of judgment we thread. Even within the circle of trust you cultivate with the grouping of the youth created, it is essential to remind them of the universe they are co-creating. We are fashioned by our culture, family values, faith, belief systems, and circle of friends. It is essential to learn to ask the right questions with the goal to discover commonalities and empathy when people appear differently from the way we are used to seeing humans in our world.

By amplifying the factors that unite us as a people, we are able to create alternative universes where the youth can create together and coexist progressively. One alternative universe we create is physical boot camps where the youth from different tribes, religions, and ideologies converge. They all have one thing in common, which is their love for the creative arts.

Through our play and performatory activities, everyone gets to know everyone else and connect in much deeper ways than they could ever imagine. This they are able to do in smaller groups. Giving them a task and deadlines helps them define a collective goal, which at that point is greater than their differences. It is their differences that then impact the quality of creative deliverables they have to develop. For instance, a stage play, a short film, a coffee-table book, a radio drama, a podcast series, or a showcase. They learn to listen and create immersive stories that align with their common goal of making a change in their communities using the creative arts.

By the time this book is published, I would have received Street Project Foundation's first award by the United Nations Alliance of Civilization and BMW Group called the Intercultural Innovation Award. It is a testament to the innovative ways by which we engage the youth from our over two hundred ethnic groups in Nigeria to interact and co-create stage performances and radio dramas that stir up conversations on social media about issues that border around social justice.

Omo, This Is Real Life, a thirteen-episode radio drama that ran on the radio is one of the creations of our youth collective. They have also been involved in the creation of a podcast series called *An ARTiculate Rant For a New Nigeria*, which is a twenty-six-episode series available across all podcast platforms. A collection of stage plays has also been created: *Play Ground, He for She, Barcode, Bolo Bolo, Mtchew: Rage of Ignorance*, and a series of short films and shows that you can find on Street Project Foundation's YouTube Channel (Street Project Foundation 2022, Watchaluv TV, 2022).

It is so essential now more than ever before that across countries of the world, we are more tolerant of each other and find less harmful ways for dialogue and consensus.

Talk to strangers.

Here is a creative exercise you can engage with your youth community to expand their worldview and be more accommodating of other people's thoughts and opinions.

CONVERSATION TAG

1. List out a number of controversial topics that may engage the youth on different pieces of paper and fold them up. Examples include: Is school a scam? What is important? Freedom of speech or freedom of religion?
2. Designate a stage area and set up two chairs there.
3. Ask for two volunteers to occupy the seats on the stage.
4. Get one of the volunteers to pick one of your folded papers randomly and read the topic aloud.
5. Give them ten to fifteen seconds for a quick reflection and prompt them to start a conversation spontaneously.
6. Ensure that other members of the youth community are present and celebrate them passionately before they commence their talk.
7. If any of the volunteers run out of things to say or struggle to contribute to the conversation, a volunteer from the

crowd can go up the stage, tap the person in question, take over their seat, and carry on with the conversation.

RULES:

1. Each party must listen with the intention to build on one another's thoughts. The goal isn't to shut each other down; the goal is to start a conversation that the youths might not always be comfortable talking about.
2. The goal isn't to question each other, so avoid asking questions during the conversation. It isn't an interview; it is a discussion.

This activity can go on for as long as the youth are comfortable. You can use your discretion to end the discussion and start a new conversation with a new set of volunteers by getting them to pick other random topics.

When the activity is over, always ask what the process was like for the youth, both those who observed and those who actively participated in the conversation. Find out what they learned.

CONCLUSION

———

Unconscious learning.

This was the best way I could describe my development as a result of my exposure to the creative arts until I came across Lois Holzman's book titled *The Overweight Brain* (Holzman, 2018). Here, she explored the concept of, "not knowing—growing."

Through improvisation, play, and performance, confidence is built and boldness to speak publicly is strengthened. Spontaneity and critical thinking, as well as team-building skills, are developed in the process. Lois Holzman corroborates this in her book which states that "the beauty and the magic of the socially created space and activity of Zones of Proximal Development are that when we are performing who we are not, learning and development happen at the very same time."

Colloquially we say, "Fake it till you make it," but I'll rephrase:

"Perform it until it
becomes your reality."

A fellow youth organizer once shared with me a story about a young man who was scared of lifts. He would rather walk many flights of stairs than get into a lift. Then an opportunity to meet with top executives of a Fortune 500 company came knocking. The location of the meeting was the top floor of a typical high-rise building in New York City. Taking that lift became inevitable. Especially as the possibility to intern in that company was also in the works.

This was an inner-city youth from a poor community in one of the boroughs of New York, and this exposure was valuable to him. With the support of his youth leader and fellow youth like himself, he prepped for this moment. His youth leader told him, "Now it's time to perform yourself going to the top floor. Think of yourself on a stage reenacting a role of a young man well dressed and going to the top floor."

He dressed for the part and had imagined himself in the lift many times before it actually happened. It was a mixture of fear and anxiety and against his sense of judgment, he got into the lift acting like he had done it before.

It wasn't an easy experience the first time and even the second time. However, the more he performed, the more accustomed he became. This is what the creative arts do. It takes you to the next level of development before you realize that growth has taken place.

Lois Holzman is a Vygotskian. That means she aligns with the thought leadership of Lev Vygostky. She states in her book that she finds psychology without Vygostky uninspiring at best and misinforming at worst (Holzman, 2018). Vygostsky believed that this becoming activity of human development is a remarkable social and cultural accomplishment. Vygostky's sociocultural theory views human development as a socially mediated process in which children acquire their cultural values, beliefs, and problem-solving strategies through collaborative dialogues with more knowledgeable members of society. Vygotsky's theory is comprised of concepts such as culture-specific tools, private speech, and the Zone of Proximal Development. Vygotsky believed that community plays a central role in the process of "making meaning."

> "You and I become the persons we are today; we weren't born that way."
>
> —LOIS HOLZMAN

After reading every chapter of *Overweight Brain*, one thing rings true: We are a product of our community and the society we live in. I wasn't born a youth leader; I became a leader through the process of doing. Borrowing terms from an improvisational world, doing here could mean "mirroring" what I saw leadership modeled for me. By doing, I find purpose in the repetition of the doing activity and start "being" one with the process of doing, especially when doing an activity I love or what feels second nature to me. Then through adversity and catharsis of emotions, the character is being formed and, in the process, you constantly evolve and become what you want to be.

I gained more clarity about my development journey after immersing myself in the theory and practice of social therapeutics, which by design explores the use of performing arts tools for human development. I love this school of thought because it does not separate the process and result of one doing, being, and becoming journey. It views the tools of development as both the process and the result. I better understand why the creative arts is such an effective tool for getting the youth to learn without consciously stating this is what you've learned, and this is how I am developing.

Performing your way to development can be likened to the act of facing your fears. Just like the young man who confronted his fear of lifts, I am constantly confronting my fears by engaging with people I never thought I'll meet in my lifetime, or trying out new projects, or traveling to new places. One of the to-go performances for entrepreneurs is the sixty-second pitch. If you were meeting with a man or woman in power who can invest in your business, how would you go about it? My answer is just do it! You may not get an outcome the first or second time but the more you engage, the more introducing yourself and your company becomes second nature to you.

One of the things I love to do with the youth is giving them group tasks and crazy timelines. After they work so hard to complete the task in the shortest possible time, I am often more interested in their process than their outcome. I ask them to reflect on the process because the focus is always on the result as opposed to enjoying the process of making things happen.

Holzman in her book states that psychology as a field, with few expectations, sees development as an individual accomplishment that happens to us from the inside. A person is a self-contained, incredibly complex biological organism whose fixed internal capacities become manifest in a systematic progression unless some internal or environmental factors interfere with the "natural order of things."

Vygotsky disagrees. He isn't denying that human beings are biological individuals and that it's the form inside us where development unfolds. He reminds us that we are as much social and cultural as we are biological and as such, we create development by how we relate to each other.

She also states, "We're not just users of what came before and what's here now. We're always making something new out of what exists. We transform the very circumstances that we're in. We engage in becoming. We create our development."

Now more than ever before, we need to engage in creating our own development. I see this as an act of love and giving. It means not being silent about what goes on in the world around us. It means being present, listening to what the people in society clamor for, and co-creating what development they want to see. We may not know what the future holds but together, we can create the future we want to see.

"And since knowing scientifically is what all of us are supposed to learn to do in order to be considered smart and become successful, our everyday thinking is shaped toward seeing things as good or evil, right or wrong, mental or physical, and innate or environmental," (Holzman, 2018). This is what is called dialectic thinking.

It's important to understand that humans are not linear beings. We are complex in our thinking process and to think that our thinking is dualistic is a license to take the moral high road and create environments that are judgmental and not suitable for development.

"Institutionalising knowing underlies nearly everything that's wrong with schools" (Holzman, 2018). It's okay to not know and not be in control all the time of the where, why, when, what, and how. Schools should focus on one's ability to take what has been provided and build with it. The focus should be on the process of creating together and the results of creating together.

Doing. Being. Becoming is an improvisational theatre of the unknowable. It is a continuous process that makes one comfortable with the fact that what we are today isn't necessarily what we will be tomorrow. What is important is our ability to create with what life throws at us. Creative Arts equips human beings with curiosity, exposure, depth of thought, critical thinking, adaptability, activism, organizing, stick-to-it-ability, and human relations needed to build careers and strengthen communities. Putting creative arts at the center of development activities is a radical step toward changing the approach to pursuing the implementation of sustainable development goals. When creative arts are at the heart of a nation's agenda for development, room is being made for young people to thrive.

ACKNOWLEDGMENTS

I want to thank the individuals that supported my book. To my committed, devoted, and loving husband, Ezenwa Okoro, I love you loads. To my kindhearted brother-in-law Kelechi Okoro. To my dear uncle Chris Ukachukwu for always being interested in my progress. My ever-supportive cousins, Agbonmeire Aimufia, Benoni Briggs, and Ogonna Owu. My mentors on different levels, Ayo Otuyalo, Tunji Olugbodi, Nnenna Onyewuchi, Lois Holzman, Cathy Salit, Babatunde Durosinmi-Etti, Marian Rich, Alison Data Phido, and Carrie Lobman. My ever-present advisor and friend who introduced me to the book creator's community, Andres Marquez-Lara. My very dear friends Adeyinka Adegbayibi, Aurelie Harp, Remilekun Oluwabamise, and Chidike Oluaoha.

Performance activists, developmentalists, improvisers, and Global Play Brigadiers across borders who believe in the power of the creative arts for human development, Dan Friedman, Omar Ali, Babara Silverman, Janet Wootten, Sandy Friedman, Gwen Lowenheim, Kathryn McCoy, Elsa Dial, Victoria Hogg, Mary Fridley, Tony Perone, David Belmont, Carlos Lopez, Jeff Gordon, Randy Wilson, and Elyse Mendel.

A big thank you to the people I refer to as catalysts: the former Global Programs Manager of VOICE, Marinke van Riet, and Program Coordinator of VOICE in Nigeria, Ijeoma Okwor. To my fellow social sector developers and colleagues, Dr. Badewa Adejugbe-Williams, Badejoko Fabamise, and Christy Asala, I say thank you.

I appreciate the collective force of Chris Street and Gabrielle L. Kurlander of All-Stars Project, Executive Director of the International Society of the Performing Arts, David Baile, and member of the board of directors, Allen Moon. A member of the board of directors of the Street Project Foundation and family friend, Paul Sachs. Sherri Hope Culver of Temple University and Rebecca Fabiano. My fellow Pan-Atlantic University alumnus, Omena Abenabe. Street Project Foundation Ambassadors, TheGift Chikere and Cynthia Nwajiobi. My fellow awardee of the United Nations Alliance of Civilizations and BMW Group's Intercultural and Innovation Award, Alexander Wenzlik. Cynthia Tucker, my first Marketing and Revisions Editor.

Austen Nwaochei, my childhood friend. The unique human being that is Ike Ogbaa. My former colleague, Tosin Asafa. Communications and public speaking guru, Flo Akinbiyi. A published author from the New Degree Press family who inspired me to write, Nifemi Aluko. African Caribbean Heritage Alliance and one of the institutions that changed my life forever—the East Side Institute, New York. Thank you for the gift of social therapeutics.

I'd also like to thank the beta readers who supported my campaign and gave feedback on my writing: Lois Holzman, Babatunde Durosinmi-Etti, Cathy Salit, and Anthony Chielo. You all are the best.

Special thanks go out to God almighty, my mother Elizabeth Omovbude, my sisters Gladys and Omoye, and my brothers, Eromosele and Irabor Omovbude. My dearest sister-in-law Adanna Okoro and brother-in-law Ikemba Okoro. My father-in-law and mother-in-law, Chris and Oge Okoro. My ever-supportive Aunt Shirley Hayes for always urging me on. The Board and Staff of Street Project Foundation: Kelechi Olawoyin, Tolulope Ajayi, Wole Oguntokun, Paul Sachs, Ugo Enwereji, Eduvie Olutimayin, Chidinma Osigwe, Anthony Chielo, and James Okewu. To my dear friend Rosemary Effiong. To the residents of 5th Avenue, M Close, Festac Town for being an inspiration.

A special thank you to Roland Ricketts for creating a series of soundtracks for the book: thank you for your love. Thank you Chuma Anagbado for the cover art of the book. A big thank you to my development editor, marketing and revisions editor, Alex Pyles and Chelsea Olivia, and New Degree Press.

Words cannot adequately express my profound gratitude to you all for being there for me in the highs and lows of my journey to writing this book.

It has been a performance of a lifetime, and I am glad you were all a part of it.

APPENDIX

———

INTRODUCTION

Adedamola, John Oluwafemi, Oluwafemi, Olanrewaju Ayeni, and David. *"The Role of Creative Arts and Poverty Alleviation in Nigeria: Scientific & Technological Approaches to Mitigating the Impact of COVID-19 pandemic and its socio-economic."* Ekiti State, Nigeria: Research Gate, 2022.https://www.researchgate.net/publication/359504006_The_Role_of_Creative_Arts_and_Poverty_Alleviation_in_Nigeria.

Bradley, Lloyd. "Stevie Wonder, Festac 1977: A Unifying Moment of Transatlantic Black Pride." *The Guardian,* August 19, 2020. https://www.theguardian.com/music/2020/aug/19/stevie-wonder-festac-1977-a-unifying-moment-of-transatlantic-black-pride.

Enahoro, Eugene. "Nigeria: The Boys' Quarters Mentality." *Daily Trust,* April 16, 2013. Accessed June 13, 2022. https://allafrica.com/stories/201304160998.html.

Holzman, Lois. *The Overweight Brain: How our obsession with knowing keeps us from getting smart enough to make a better world*. New York: East Side Institute Press, 2018.

Lee, Giacomo. "Are artists 'non-essential'?" *Digital Arts,* June 15, 2020. Accessed June 13, 2022. https://www.digitalartsonline. co.uk/features/creative-business/are-artists-non-essential/.

Maikori, Yahaya. "The Nigerian Creative Economy: Its History to Date and Current Trends." *Law Allianz,* April 21, 2020. Accessed June 13, 2022. https://www.lawallianz.com/publications/the-nigerian-creative-economy-its-history-to-date-and-current-trends/.

McGregor, Jena. "The Next In-Demand Job Title: Head Of The Future Of Work." Forbes. January 18, 2022. https://www.forbes. com/sites/jenamcgregor/2022/01/18/the-next-in-demand-job-title-head-of-the-future-of-work/?sh=3e08b10360b8.

Migiro, Geoffery. "Traditional Nigerian Clothing." World Atlas. August 1, 2019. Accessed June 26, 2022. https://www.worldatlas. com/articles/traditional-nigerian-clothing.html.

Obama, Barack. *The Promised Land.* New York: Penguin Random House, 2020.

Oluwole, Victor. "New Report Shows Nigeria's Creative Industry Is the Country's Second-Largest Employer and Has the Potential to Produce 2.7million Jobs by 2025." *Business Insider,* May 10, 2021. https://africa.businessinsider.com/local/lifestyle/new-report-shows-nigerias-creative-industry-is-the-countrys-second-largest-employer/mky68v9.

Street Project Foundation. "Home." Accessed June 26, 2022. https://streetproject.org.ng/.

The Lego Group. "LEGO Group Kicks Off Global Program To Inspire The Next Generation Of Space Explorers As NASA Celebrates 50 Years Of Moon Landing." *Cision PR News Wire,* July 16, 2019. Accessed June 26, 2022. https://www.prnewswire.com/news-releases/lego-group-kicks-off-global-program-to-inspire-the-next-generation-of-space-explorers-as-nasa-celebrates-50-years-of-moon-landing-300885423.html.

CHAPTER ONE

Alyanna, Nikki. "Avoidance Key to Survival or Destruction?"- *Mental Health and Addictions Community | Medium* (blog), August 28, 2020. https://medium.com/mental-health-and-addictions-community/avoidance-key-to-survival-or-destruction-7b407451259d.

Economic Commission for Africa. *Africa's Youth and Prospects for Inclusive Development.* Addis Ababa: United Nations, Economic Commission for Africa, February 2017. Accessed June 26, 2022. https://www.ohchr.org/sites/default/files/Documents/Issues/Youth/UNEconomicCommissionAfrica.pdf.

Iwenjora, Fred. "Maryam Babangida Still Lives in Boy Who Mesmerised Her with Xylophone." *Vanguard News,* December 20, 2019. Accessed June 26, 2022. https://www.vanguardngr.com/2019/12/maryam-babangida-still-lives-in-boy-who-mesmerised-her-with-xylophone/.

Kapusta, Michelle. "Who Tyler Perry's Famous Madea Character Is Really Based off Of." Showbiz Cheat Sheet. February 18, 2022. https://www.cheatsheet.com/entertainment/tyler-perrys-famous-madea-character-really-based-off.html/.

Modesitt, L.E., Jr. "Parachutes and Sir James Dewar." L.E. Modesitt, Jr. January 12, 2016. Accessed June 26, 2022. https://www.lemodesittjr.com/2016/01/12/parachutes-and-sir-james-dewar/.

Noah, Trevor. *Born a Crime: Stories from a South African Childhood.* New York: Spiegel & Grau, 2016.

Vinney, Cynthia. "Cultivation Theory." *ThoughtCo* (blog), October 23, 2019. https://www.thoughtco.com/cultivation-theory-definition-4588455.

Winfrey, Oprah. "Oprah Talks to Tyler Perry." Oprah.com. November 16, 2010. Accessed June 26, 2022. https://www.oprah.com/entertainment/oprah-interviews-tyler-perry_1/all.

CHAPTER TWO

Allende, Isabelle. "Isabel Allende Quotes." BrainyQuote. Accessed June 25, 2022. https://www.brainyquote.com/quotes/isabel_allende_599161.

East Side Institute. "About - Social Therapeutics." Accessed March 8, 2022. https://eastsideinstitute.org/about/social-therapeutics/.

Moses-Ashike, Hope and Emelike Obinna. "What to Expect as National Theatre Gets N21bn Makeover."*Businessday NG*, April

25, 2022. https://businessday.ng/news/article/what-to-expect-as-national-theatre-gets-n21bn-makeover/.

Ochayi, Chris. "40% Of Nigerian Youths Jobless; Angry, Restless - Adesina." *Vanguard News*, March 1, 2022. https://www.vanguardngr.com/2022/03/40-of-nigerian-youths-jobless-angry-restless-adesina/.

Performing the World. "Who We Are." Accessed June 26, 2022. https://www.performingtheworld.org/who-we-are.

Street Project Foundation. "Home." Accessed June 26, 2022. https://streetproject.org.ng/.

Winfrey, Oprah. "Oprah Winfrey Quote." Love Expands. Accessed July 3, 2022. https://loveexpands.com/quotes/oprah-winfrey-1224000/.

Wood, Anthony. "'Vision without Action Is a Daydream. Action without Vision Is a Nightmare.'" *Pinnacle Traction* (blog), November 6, 2020. https://www.pinnacletraction.com.au/vision-without-action-is-a-daydream-action-without-vision-is-a-nightmare-is-a-famous-japanese-proverb-and-addressing-this-balance-in-organisations-is-how-i-spend-a-lot-of-my-time/.

CHAPTER THREE

Chiiya, Chipo, Mutale Chonta, Sue Clay, Ross Kidd, and Petra Röhr-Rouendaal. "We Are All in the Same Boat! Using Art and Creative Approaches with Young People to Tackle HIV-Related Stigma." Unesdoc | Unesdoc Digital Library, 2007. https://unesdoc.unesco.org/ark:/48223/pf0000189249.

Cronkleton, Emily. "10 Breathing Exercises to Try: For Stress, Training & Lung Capacity." *Healthline*, April 9, 2019. https://www.healthline.com/health/breathing-exercise#pursed-lip-breathing.

Crossroads Hospice Charitable Foundation. "How Arts and Crafts Help Children Express Grief." Crossroads Hospice Charitable Foundation. September 24, 2015. https://crhcf.org/insights/how-arts-and-crafts-help-children-express-grief/.

DePaul, Kristi. "What Does It Really Take to Build a New Habit?" *Harvard Business Review*, February 2, 2021. https://hbr.org/2021/02/what-does-it-really-take-to-build-a-new-habit.

Ezenwa-Okoro, Rita. "Dealing with Loss. A deep conversation with StephREDD." Facebook (Video), March 5, 2021. https://www.facebook.com/rita.omovbude/videos/10159418969694047?_rdc=1&_rdr.

Gidlund, Jeanne M. "Art Therapy and Other Creative Modalities Used for Children/Adolescents Suffering from Grief." Dissertation, Minds@UW, 2018. https://minds.wisconsin.edu/bitstream/handle/1793/78499/GidlundArt%20Therapy%20and%20Other%20Modalities%20Used%20for%20Grief.pdf.

GoodTherapy Editor. "Art Therapy." GoodTherapy. April 18, 2016. https://www.goodtherapy.org/learn-about-therapy/types/art-therapy.

Jakes, T.D. "Quotable Quotes." Quotes. Goodreads. Accessed July 3, 2022. https://www.goodreads.com/quotes/778709-never-make-a-permanent-decision-about-a-temporary-situation.

Martin, Brittany Harker. "Brain Research Shows the Arts Promote Mental Health." *The Conversation*, June 9, 2020. https://theconversation.com/brain-research-shows-the-arts-promote-mental-health-136668.

Merton, Thomas. *No Man Is an Island*. New York: Houghton Mifflin Harcourt Publishing Company, 1955.

Mitchell, Douglas. "How Art Heals." *Good Therapy* (blog), March 27, 2012. https://www.goodtherapy.org/blog/how-art-heals-grief-0327125/.

Stanford University. "The Role of Creativity and the Arts in a 21st-Century Education." *Stanford News*, April 20, 2006. https://news.stanford.edu/news/2006/april26/hentext-042606.html.

Ogbo, Keno. "The Delusion of Clocks." *Illumination | Medium* (blog), May 4, 2021. https://medium.com/illumination/the-delusion-of-clocks-5658a9503f3.

Slate, Candice N. and Scott, David A. *A discussion of coping methods and counseling techniques for children and adults dealing with grief and bereavement*. Charlotte, NC: American Counseling Association Annual Conference and Exposition, 2019. Accessed June 26, 2022. https://www.counseling.org/resources/library/vistas/2009-V-pt.2/Slate-Scott.doc.

UNESCO. *"We Are All in the Same Boat! Using Art and Creative Approaches with Young People to Tackle HIV Related Stigma."* Spain: UNESDOC Digital Library, 2010. Accessed June 26, 2022. https://unesdoc.unesco.org/ark:/48223/pf0000189249.

CHAPTER FOUR

Jones, Luvvie Ajayi. "Get Comfortable with Being Uncomfortable." Filmed December 2017 in Vancouver, Canada. TED Video, 10:45. https://www.ted.com/talks/luvvie_ajayi_jones_get_comfortable_with_being_uncomfortable.

Ogunbiyi, Michael Temitope. "Directorial Style and Stylization: 'the Photographic Synthesis' in Felix Okolo's dramaturgy on the Nigerian theatre stage." *EJOTMAS: Ekpoma Journal of Theatre and Media Arts* Vol. 5, No. 1-2 (2015): 1-25. http://dx.doi.org/10.4314/ejotmas.v5i1-2.1

Rev (blog). "Reverend Al Sharpton Eulogy Transcript at George Floyd's Memorial Service." June 4, 2020. Accessed July 7, 2022. https://www.rev.com/blog/transcripts/reverend-al-sharpton-eulogy-transcript-at-george-floyd-memorial-service#fl-main-content.sharpton-eulogy-transcript-at-george-floyd-memorial-service#fl-main-content.

Shakespeare, William. *As You like It*. Ware: Penguin Classics, 1599.

Williamson, Marianne. *A Return to Love: Reflections on the Principles of a Course in Miracles*. New York: HarperCollins Publishers, 1992.

CHAPTER FIVE

East Side Institute. Initiatives - Play, Development & Social Justice. July 20, 2021. https://eastsideinstitute.org/play-development-social-justice/.

Ezenwa-Okoro, Rita. "Thought Splurge." Mysite. Accessed June 24, 2022. https://www.onlinewithreo.com/thought-splurge.

FAO. "Urgent Action Needed to Stop Child Labour in Africa as Covid-19 Pushes More Children into Work." *ReliefWeb*, September 29, 2021. https://reliefweb.int/report/world/urgent-action-needed-stop-child-labour-africa-covid-19-pushes-more-children-work.

France-Presse, Agence. "18.5 Million Nigerian Children Are out of School, UNICEF Says." *VOA*, May 12, 2022. https://www.voanews.com/a/millions-nigerian-children-are-out-of-school-unicef-says/6569716.html.

Goodman, Stacey. "11 Ways to Help Students Overcome Creative Blocks." Edutopia (blog) George Lucas Educational Foundation, May 19, 2015. Accessed June 26, 2022. https://www.edutopia.org/blog/11-ways-help-students-overcome-creative-blocks-stacey-goodman.

Haltiwanger, John. "Trump Doesn't Deny Calling African Countries 'Shitholes' While Meeting with Nigeria's President." *Business Insider*, April 30, 2018. https://www.businessinsider.com/trump-doesnt-deny-calling-african-countries-shitholes-2018-4.

Keys, Alicia. *Underdog*. RCA Records and Sony Music Entertainment. January 9, 2020. https://genius.com/Alicia-keys-underdog-lyrics.

Mitti Cafe. "*Home*," Accessed June 26, 2022. https://www.mitticafe.org/.

Mureithi, Carlos. "African Nonprofits Want to 'Decolonize' Donor Funding." *Quartz*, September 30, 2021. https://qz.com/africa/2066091/african-nonprofits-want-to-decolonize-donor-funding/.

"Nigeria Population (Live)." Worldometer. Accessed June 29, 2022. https://www.worldometers.info/world-population/nigeria-population/.

Oluwole, Victor. "Nigeria Is No Longer the Poverty Capital of the World but Still Has over 70 Million People Living in Extreme Poverty - the Highest in Africa." *Business Insider Africa*, March 10, 2022. https://africa.businessinsider.com/local/markets/nigeria-is-no-longer-the-poverty-capital-of-the-world-but-still-has-over-70-million/2txm7g3.

Pajer, Nicole. "Adults Need Playtime as Much as Kids." *Shondaland*, November 2, 2021. https://www.shondaland.com/live/body/a36123122/adults-need-playtime-as-much-as-kids/.

Rich, Marian. *"Home."* Accessed June 29, 2022. https://www.marianrich.com/.

Salit, Cathy. Performance Breakthrough: A Radical Approach to Success at Work. New York: Hachette Books, 2016

Schoch, Martha, and Christoph Lakner. "The Number of Poor People Continues to Rise in Sub-Saharan Africa, despite a Slow Decline in the Poverty Rate." *World Bank Blogs* (blog), December 16, 2020. https://blogs.worldbank.org/opendata/number-poor-people-continues-rise-sub-saharan-africa-despite-slow-decline-poverty-rate.

TEDx Talks. "MITTI - Celebrating Ability in Disability." March 17, 2020. Video, 16:02. https://www.youtube.com/watch?v=K-dO8miPWfAE.

World Meter. *Nigerian Population (Live)."* Accessed July 6, 2022. https://www.worldometers.info/world-population/nigeria-population/.

CHAPTER SIX

Adaoyichie, Goodness. "'Rejecting #Nottooyoungtorun Bill Will Be Political Suicide' Says Youth Group." *Pulse Nigeria*, March 14, 2018. Accessed July 2, 2022. https://www.pulse.ng/news/politics/buhari-rejecting-nottooyoungtorun-bill-will-be-political-suicide-says-youth-group/l1cfjdk.

Adefarasin, Paul. "A Quote by Paul Adefarasin." Goodreads. Goodreads. Accessed July 3, 2022. https://www.goodreads.com/quotes/895801-excuse-is-the-tool-of-the-incompetent-a-monument-of.

Black Lives Matter. 2021. "Herstory." Black Lives Matter Retrieved May 2021. https://blacklivesmatter.com/herstory.

Channels Television. "President Buhari Signs Not-Too-Young-to-Run Bill into Law." May 31, 2018. Video, 1:01. https://www.youtube.com/watch?v=a71DhB_WT7o.

Ebunike, Nwanchukwu. "Framing the #Occupy Nigeria Protests in Newspapers and Social Media." Scientific Research Open Access Vol. 02 (May, 2015): 1-13. https://www.scirp.org/html/68376_68376.htm.

Egbas, Jude. "How Young Nigerians Forced President to Agree on Bill." *Pulse Nigeria,* May 31, 2018. Accessed July 2, 2022. https://www.pulse.ng/news/politics/buhari-how-young-nigerians-forced-president-to-agree-on-bill/l34gkj3.

Freelon, Deen, Charlton McIlwain, and Meredith Clark. 2018. "Quantifying the Power and Consequences of Social Media Protest." New Media & Society 20(3): 990–1011 https://journals.sagepub.com/doi/abs/10.1177/1461444816676646.

Kabir, Adejumo. "10 Reasons #Endsars Protest Gained Global Attention - Premium Times Nigeria." *Premium Times Nigeria - Premium Times* November 7, 2020. https://www.premiumtimesng.com/news/top-news/425026-10-reasons-endsars-protest-gained-global-attention.html.

Mark, Monica. "Nigeria Reels after Oil Subsidy Row Turns into Country's Biggest Ever Protest." *The Guardian,* January 18, 2012. Accessed July 2, 2022. https://www.theguardian.com/world/2012/jan/18/nigeria-power-struggle-protest-oil.

Nwakanma, Adaugo Pamela. "From Black Lives Matter to Endsars: Women's Socio-Political Power and the Transnational Movement for Black Lives: Perspectives on Politics." Cambridge University Press, Volume 20 Number 2 (March, 2022): 1-14. https://www.cambridge.org/core/journals/perspectives-on-politics/article/abs/from-black-lives-matter-to-endsars-womens-sociopolitical-power-and-the-transnational-movement-for-black-lives/5B65728A08EEE5764326CD180681FCF5.

Salaudeen, Aisha-nana. "Fw: What about the Not Too Young to Run Bill?" *Stears Business,* June 4, 2018. Accessed June 26,

2022. https://www.stearsng.com/article/fw-what-about-the-not-too-young-to-run-bill/.

Shryock, Ricci. "Occupy Nigeria Movement Says It Won't Stop Fighting Government Corruption." *VOA*, January 10, 2012. Accessed June 26, 2022. https://www.voanews.com/a/occupy-nigeria-movement-says-it-wont-stop-fighting-government-waste-137031473/159429.html.

Sowore, Omoyele. "Opinion: Nigerians Still Waiting for Their 'African Spring'." *CNN*, January 14, 2013. Accessed July 2, 2022. https://edition.cnn.com/2013/01/12/world/africa/nigeria-protests-african-spring/index.html.

CHAPTER SEVEN

Anyadike, Ikenna Chidiebere. "Why Are Youth Safe Spaces Important?" Atlas Corps, July 6, 2020. https://atlascorps.org/why-are-youth-safe-spaces-important/.

Eisler, Melissa. "10 Ways to Create an Environment That Fosters Creativity." *Melissa Eisler*, August 17, 2021. https://melissaeisler.com/10-ways-to-create-a-team-environment-that-fosters-creative-thinking/.

Fayehun, Funke and Uche Charlie Isiugo-Abanihe. "#Endsars: How Nigeria Can Tap into Its Youthful Population." *The Conversation*, April 20, 2022. https://theconversation.com/endsars-how-nigeria-can-tap-into-its-youthful-population-148319.

Ford Foundation. "Nigeria Youth Futures Fund Will Equip a New Cadre of Youth Leaders in the Region." Ford Foundation news

release, September 13, 2021. https://www.fordfoundation.org/
news-and-stories/news-and-press/news/nigeria-youth-futures-
fund-will-equip-a-new-cadre-of-youth-leaders-in-the-region/.

Siltanen, Rob. "Quotable Quotes." Goodreads. Accessed July 7,
2022. https://www.goodreads.com/quotes/924-here-s-to-the-
crazy-ones-the-misfits-the-rebels-the.

Texas Beeworks. "Backyard Shed Full of Bees, March 2021." March
11, 2021. Video, 4:29. https://www.youtube.com/watch?v=a_
VBqXouGgE.

Youth Power 2. "Safe Public Spaces for Youth." USAID. Accessed
July 3, 2022. https://www.youthpower.org/safe-spaces-youth.

CHAPTER EIGHT

Backyard Brains. "Experiment: How fast your brain reacts to
stimuli." Accessed June 24, 2022. https://backyardbrains.com/
experiments/reactiontime.

Gregoire, Carolyn. "Understanding the Four Stages of the Creative
Process." *We Work Ideas* (blog), October 18, 2019. https://www.
wework.com/ideas/professional-development/creativity-cul-
ture/understanding-the-four-stages-of-the-creative-process.

Hoteit, Leila. "3 Lessons on Success from an Arab Businesswoman."
Filmed July 2016 in BCG Paris. TED Video, 13:53. https://www.
ted.com/talks/leila_hoteit_3_lessons_on_success_from_an_
arab_businesswoman.

Ju, Anne. "Courage Is the Most Important Virtue, Says Writer and Civil Rights Activist Maya Angelou at Convocation." *Cornell Chronicle,* May 24, 2008. Accessed June 29, 2022. https://news.cornell.edu/stories/2008/05/courage-most-important-virtue-maya-angelou-tells-seniors.

Koyenikan, Idowu. "Wealth for All: Living a Life of Success at the Edge of Your Ability." Networking Skills Quotes. Goodreads. January 11, 2016. https://www.goodreads.com/quotes/tag/networking-skills.

Leonard, Michael. "Use These Powerful Visualization Quotes to Create a Beautiful Future." *Fearless Soul* (blog), July 19, 2018. https://iamfearlesssoul.com/powerful-visualization-quotes/.

CHAPTER NINE

Ezenwa-Okoro, Rita. Online with REO, Instagram. May 29, 2020. https://www.instagram.com/tv/CAxyDkpp3wk/?igshid=YmMyMTA2M2Y%3D.

Human Rights Watch. "Nigeria: People with Mental Health Conditions Chained, Abused." November 11, 2019. https://www.hrw.org/news/2019/11/11/nigeria-people-mental-health-conditions-chained-abused.

Iwalaiye, Temi. "The Unnoticed Prevalence of Suicide in Nigeria." *Pulse Nigeria,* September 14, 2021. https://www.pulse.ng/lifestyle/the-unnoticed-prevalence-of-suicide-in-nigeria/70g6280.

Mental Health America. "Racism and Mental Health." Accessed June 29, 2022. https://www.mhanational.org/racism-and-mental-health.

NSW Legislation. Mental Health Act. New South Wales: 1958. https://legislation.nsw.gov.au/view/pdf/asmade/act-1958-45.

Salaudeen, Aisha. "Chained and Locked up, Why Some Nigerians Turn to Religion First to Treat the Mentally Ill." *CNN*, October 10, 2020. Accessed June 29, 2022. https://edition.cnn.com/2020/10/10/africa/mental-health-religious-treatment-nigeria/index.html.

The Guardian. "Latest News from around the World." Accessed June 29, 2022. https://www.theguardian.com/world.

White, Taneasha. "Art Therapy for Trauma: Here's How It Can Help." Psych Central. May 19, 2022. https://psychcentral.com/ptsd/art-therapy-for-trauma.

CHAPTER TEN

Adichie, Chimamanda Ngozi. "The Danger of a Single Story" Filmed October 2009 at TED Global. TED Video, 18:33. https://www.ted.com/talks/chimamanda_ngozi_adichie_the_danger_of_a_single_story?language=en.

BBC Radio 4. "Radio 4 in Four - Why We Should All Talk to Strangers." TV. Accessed June 24, 2022. https://www.bbc.co.uk/programmes/articles/d1q6FmHxf1t2wKkprp4XvG/why-we-should-all-talk-to-strangers.

Covey, Stephen R. *The 7 Habits of Highly Effective People*. London: Simon & Schuster, 2004.

Lake, Monica. "The Importance of Social Skills: Raising a Socially Intelligent Child." *Good Therapy Blog*, January 2, 2018. Accessed June 29, 2022. https://www.goodtherapy.org/blog/importance-of-social-skills-raising-socially-intelligent-child-0102184.

Learning Portal Team. "The Power of Social and Emotional Skills." *Unesco IIEP Learning Portal* (blog), March 7, 2018. https://learningportal.iiep.unesco.org/en/blog/the-power-of-social-and-emotional-skills.

Quotefancy. "Pope John XXIII Quote: 'What Unites Us, Is Much Greater than What Divides Us.'" Accessed June 29, 2022. https://quotefancy.com/quote/1259155/Pope-John-XXIII-What-unites-us-is-much-greater-than-what-divides-us.

Stark, Kio. *When Strangers Meet: How People You Don't Know, Can Transform You*. London: Simon & Schuster, 2016.

Street Project Foundation. "*Street University*." Accessed July 6, 2022. https://streetproject.org.ng/street-university/.

TED. "Why you should talk to strangers | Kio Stark." September 23, 2016. Video, 11:52. https://www.youtube.com/watch?v=rF-pDK2KhAgw.

Watchaluv TV. "Videos." Accessed July 6, 2022. https://www.youtube.com/channel/UC46inZGbK4fQOCSlVBG3v6g/videos.

CONCLUSION

Holzman, Lois. *The Overweight Brain: How our obsession with knowing keeps us from getting smart enough to make a better world.* New York: East Side Institute Press, 2018.

CPSIA information can be obtained
at www.ICGtesting.com
Printed in the USA
JSHW050331200323
39031JS00006B/11